CLARITY QUEST

How to Take a Sabbatical Without Taking More Than a Week Off

Pamela Ammondson

A FIRESIDE BOOK
Published by Simon & Schuster

To my father, mother, and husband, Karl

Thank you for your wise guidance,
continued support, and love

FIRESIDE
Rockefeller Center
1230 Avenue of the Americas
New York, NY 10020

FIRESIDE and colophon are registered trademarks
of Simon & Schuster Inc.

Designed by Irving Perkins Associates

Manufactured in the United States of America

10   9   8   7   6   5   4   3   2

Library of Congress Cataloging-in-Publication Data
Ammondson, Pamela.
     Clarity quest : how to take a sabbatical without taking more than a week
off / Pamela Ammondson.
         p.   cm.
     1. Change (Psychology)   2. Quality of life.   I. Title.
     BF637.C4A48   1999
     158.1—dc21   99-17990
                                                                        CIP

ISBN 0-684-86320-0

Acknowledgments

My heartfelt appreciation to Connie Johnson, Bill Coyle, Kathy Salmonson, John Gibbons, Bill Watson, Toni Marshall Cole, Bob and Jan Briggs, Todd Ourston, Magee Hemmer, Gay Luce, Nancy Coughlan, Carol Costello, my clients and colleagues, and the Clarity Quest Pioneers. Thank you for sharing your insights, ideas, and experiences, and helping to refine and improve Clarity Quest. I'm also grateful to other supportive friends and family: Greg and Karen Moore, Kathy Ruby, Marlie Rowell, Sandy Sanchez, Karl and Hylda Kachigan, my grandmother, Shirley, and sisters, Debbie Ammondson, and Rhonda Anderson. I thank you for your encouragement and love. A BIG thank you to Joe Matthews for his friendship, ongoing support, and for the many hours he spent reading drafts of the manuscript and providing valuable feedback; Carolyn Kellams for her optimism, loving support, and rays of sunshine, especially on cloudy days, and to Irene Economou for her gifts of insights, understanding, and love.

A special thanks to my agent, Sarah Jane Freymann, for her wisdom and wonderful guidance; and to my editor, Sarah Baker, for her faith, infectious enthusiasm, and inspiration. My gratitude also goes to Becky Cabaza, Carrie Thornton, Ghena Glijansky, and all the others at Fireside for editorial suggestions and production help. My deepest appreciation goes to God and to the many wonderful teachers who taught me the principles of Clarity Quest: Dr. McKee, Frannie Hamil, Sepp Morscher, inspiring writers, speakers, and guides. All have enriched my life and I am very grateful!

Contents

Part Three
REACHING THE SUMMIT

Introduction

⛭ This book is for all the people who long for time to reflect, revitalize, and refocus their lives but can't afford a full-fledged sabbatical. If you are stressed out, burned out, or simply out of energy and fresh ideas, this book will show you how to recharge your batteries, assess what's genuinely important in your life, and rediscover who you are and what you really want.

I started writing *Clarity Quest* to a dear friend who was very unhappy in her job. It actually began as a drawing and a few bullet points on a napkin.

I'd met my friend for a walk on a beautiful August evening. We hiked through a grove of redwoods and discovered, at the top of a hill, a breathtaking view of the bay and the valley below. It was dusk, and the light was soft and golden. The pine-scented air was very still, and house lights were just coming on. They looked like distant stars twinkling in the valley below. We stopped for a few minutes to admire this wonderful panorama. It was beautiful and very peaceful.

After a few moments of silence, I turned to my friend. She was clearly not at peace, even in this beautiful, tranquil setting. Worry lines were etched on her forehead. She looked extremely tired and distraught.

She told me she was mentally, emotionally, and physically exhausted from working at a very stressful job that she didn't enjoy — but that she was terrified of losing. Her company had recently reorganized, and she was doing work that had previously kept two people busy. The daily meetings, long hours, and work-related problems had completely drained her. Nevertheless, she worried that if she worked fewer hours and didn't complete all her tasks, she'd be the next person to be laid off. She was so fearful that she had a hard time sleeping at night. Even her dreams were job related. She dreamed that she was on a treadmill, running as fast as she could and unable to adjust the speed or get off.

Her job stress had started to affect other areas of her life. She began drinking more coffee, just to keep alert, and started eating at her desk to save time—mostly unhealthy vending machine foods loaded with sugar and preservatives. She quit her exercise class after work so she could put in a few extra hours, and stopped going out with friends in the evening because she was too tired. At the end of the day, she barely had enough energy to microwave a frozen dinner or to stay awake for a television program. Her relationship with her partner suffered, and she stopped enjoying life's simple pleasures—beauty, joy, laughter, and love.

As much as she disliked her job, she couldn't see how to restructure it and couldn't face the prospect of looking for another one. Basically, she was too tired and too fearful to think at all.

I was very saddened by my friend's state of mind. Her lifestyle and attitude had changed dramatically under these stressful working conditions. She was only forty years old and felt that she had reached a dead end in her career and her life. She felt stuck and didn't know how to get unstuck. She had no hope, no dreams, and no life beyond her current job.

My friend was paying a very high price for remaining in a job that she didn't enjoy.

PRESCRIPTION FOR A FRIEND

We talked about her dilemma on our way down the hill. The walking and talking helped, but it wasn't enough to reenergize her. She was like a car whose batteries are nearly drained, that is low on fuel, and that desperately needs a tune-up. She was depleted and wasn't going to perform at her best until she recharged, refueled, and tuned up.

By the time we finished our walk, it was completely dark and I suggested we continue our talk in a nearby café. I asked the waiter for a pen and drew a mountain on a paper napkin. At the top I wrote *Rx for a Friend: Clarity Quest.*

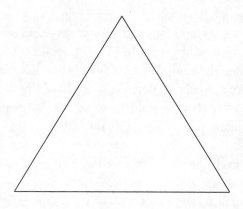

While the memory of hiking up the hill was still fresh in her mind, I asked my friend to visualize the view from on top of a very high mountain. At the summit she would be able to see clearly in all directions. She would see things from a higher perspective and in their true relative importance to one another. I used the example of reaching the summit as a metaphor for what she needed to do in her life. She needed to rise above her fears so that she had an unobstructed view and could see clearly what changes she needed to make in her life.

To get beyond her fearful state, she first needed to renew, restore, and recharge her energy. She could then reach the top of her mountain with a clear and alert mind and focus on what she needed to change in her job and her life in order to make both more satisfying.

I outlined the eight-week Clarity Quest program on the napkin and promised that if she followed it, she would gain the personal strength and inner power necessary to get back in control of her life.

PERSONAL QUEST FOR CLARITY

I came to discover this process while undergoing my own professional, personal, health, and financial crises. I had left a very secure corporate job and founded a home services business. I soon realized that I hated running this business, and at the same time I found myself in the middle of a divorce that left me financially strapped, emotionally vulnerable, and physically ill with an intestinal disorder. I was afraid to close the business because I needed the money, and grew more miserable, confused, and fearful by the day.

For the next three years I explored ways to get physically, financially, psychologically, and professionally healthy—and walked myself through a long version of what became Clarity Quest. I spent hours reading books, researching medical and health issues, taking classes, and seeking advice from psychologists, doctors, nutritionists, fitness experts, family, and friends. My life was way out of balance. I knew I had to make some drastic changes, but I was too tired to focus and concentrate. The thought of visualizing, setting goals, and achieving them made me even more exhausted. I simply didn't have the energy to think clearly, and I felt claustrophobic.

Ancient wisdom suggests that the answers are within us. We just need to be quiet in order to hear them. My problem was that I couldn't hear that "still, small voice" because so many other things were screaming for my attention—including an unhealthy body.

I remember joking with friends about renting a room at the state mental hospital near my home. It had beautiful grounds with manicured lawns and large, sweeping oak trees. Patients would sit outside in old white lawn chairs. Believe it or not, this setting appealed to me because I was dying to escape life's fast pace for a while.

Deep inside, I knew that the faster I could get back into a healthy state of mind and body, the faster I would know how to change my life. But I didn't know how to get healthier. I was consumed by pressing deadlines to meet, clients to call, employees to talk to, and finances to worry about. I didn't want to run off and become a monk, and I couldn't afford a vacation to a spa.

I realized that it had to come down to me. I needed to take control of my own destiny. So I began taking care of myself. I started eating healthy and nutritious foods, learned how to relax, exercised, and worked to eliminate some of my unproductive fears.

I also retreated to the outdoors. Being outside was like a homecoming for me, since I'd grown up in Montana and knew how renewing, restorative, and healing the powers of nature could be. Whenever I was distressed when I was young, I'd escape down to the river at sunset or find a grove of trees where I could just sit and be still. The quiet and beauty calmed my mind and helped me access my inner wisdom, although at the time I was unaware of what was happening.

Finally I did achieve what I had set out to do. I had renewed my spirit, uncluttered my mind, and found clarity. I was able to identify the job of my dreams, the qualities I was looking for in a mate, the type of car I wanted to own, and even what my dream house looked like—light and airy, with an office, a garden, and hardwood floors in the kitchen. I wrote everything down in great detail, and remarkable things started to happen! I ran a marathon, paid off my debts, purchased a beautiful brand-new convertible, married a wonderful man, and landed a perfect new job without even making a phone call!

Some friends remarked that I'd gotten lucky. I knew that it wasn't just luck.

Four years later I had to repeat the Clarity Quest process. I was working as a communications consultant in charge of Hewlett-Packard's satellite television operation in northern California when Hewlett-Packard downsized and eliminated a number of positions, including mine. This time I knew exactly what to do! I followed the principles that are outlined in this book and was able to revitalize, take stock, and quickly find the new job of my dreams. I founded my own communications consulting company and now work with Fortune 500 companies as well as start-up companies and individuals.

I shared my Clarity Quest process with many friends, colleagues, and clients who found themselves in a similar situation to where I had been. Through working with them, I streamlined the process and found ways to help people focus more quickly. I started teaching workshops and helped people clear away the anxiety, fear, exhaustion, insecurity, unhealthy emotions, and mental clutter that kept them from enjoying their lives. They were able to focus on what they *really* wanted and take control of their lives with a new sense of purpose and vision. You'll read several inspiring stories of people who have been through the program. I know their stories will motivate you and show you how easily you can gain control of your life. You can feel healthier and better about yourself, break free of analysis paralysis, get clear about what you want, and create your best possible life and livelihood.

ENJOY THE BENEFITS OF A SABBATICAL

Many people get excited when they discover that they can enjoy the benefits of a sabbatical—revitalizing and refocusing their careers and personal lives—without spending a lot of time, energy, and money. Most of us simply don't have the luxury of time to step off the treadmill and reassess our lives. We struggle with the demands of work, family, and social pressures and wonder how we can possibly squeeze one more minute out of our hectic schedules. We try to plan vacation time to refresh the soul and clear the mind, but we're so busy in the weeks leading up to the vacation that we spend the entire time simply trying to slow down, relax, and catch up on our sleep. It's hard to do serious thinking and structured planning when you're stressed out and tired.

The Clarity Quest program allows you to take a much-needed sabbatical, and you only have to take one week off!

During the first seven weeks in your preparation for the sabbatical, you'll find that you restore your energy quickly and gain the strength, stamina, and calm you need to make important career and life decisions. Each week you'll work on a new activity, building on the previous week. You'll find the process has its own momentum. The activities can fit into even the busiest schedules and will help you feel better about yourself and more in control. By week eight you'll be able to think clearly and creatively during your week-long getaway. And the moment you clarify what you want, magical things will begin to happen. Best of luck on your Quest!

Chapter 1

Clarity Quest Fundamentals

▦ It's time to step back, relax, restore, and regenerate while you rethink your profession and your life in a structured way.

THE CLARITY QUEST PROGRAM

The goal of this program is to renew your physical, emotional, mental, and spiritual energy so that you can think clearly and make new choices about your life and future.

During the first weeks of Clarity Quest, you'll start to restore health, build strength and stamina, and calm fears. Since mountain climbing is so popular, I thought *summiting* would be a good metaphor for how the program is organized. You'll work to get physically, mentally, and spiritually fit so that you can make it to the top with a fresh perspective and a clear view of the future.

The first few weeks you undergo Base Camp Training. Then, with new reserves of energy, you'll spend the next three weeks Lightening Your Load—pulling in scattered energies, cleansing unhealthy emotions, and learning to nourish your soul. During the final week you'll take your own personal Clarity Quest, a five- to seven-day getaway to a beautiful place where you'll begin to define a new, more satisfying life. By then you'll have all the tools you need to know just what you want from your job and your life. You'll develop a clear vision of what you want to do—and then formulate an action plan to turn that dream into reality.

Each of the eight weeks is organized around one aspect of this process, with specific written exercises, outdoor activities, focused getaways, and other guidelines to clear away the cobwebs. It's fun and simple, I promise!

PART 1. BASE CAMP TRAINING

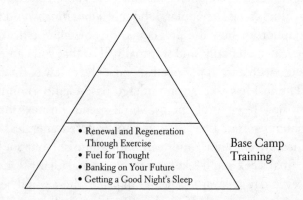

Week 1. Getting a Good Night's Sleep

This is a week to catch up on your sleep, relax, unwind, and get enough rest to restore vital energy. Exercises help quiet the mind and keep stress under control. A five-step plan ensures restful sleep.

Week 2. Banking on Your Future

Finances are the greatest source of stress for most people. This week you'll put together the facts and figures you need to develop your own personal financial plan. You'll turn amorphous worry into manageable numbers and an action plan that gives you peace of mind. Whatever changes you choose to make in your life, you'll know exactly how much money you need to survive. During this week you'll experience activities that make you feel joyful and abundant but cost little or nothing.

Week 3. Fuel for Thought

Exercises help you determine what types of mind and body fuel make you feel sluggish, and what types of mind and body fuel make you feel energized and revitalized. You'll develop a simple eating plan that will keep both your body and mind satiated.

Week 4. Renewal and Regeneration Through Exercise

This week is about learning how exercise can calm fears, reduce stress, increase energy, and promote physical well-being. You'll learn how to get started exercising and how to stick with a program.

PART 2. LIGHTENING THE LOAD

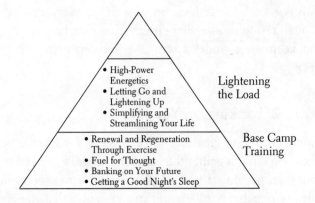

- High-Power Energetics
- Letting Go and Lightening Up
- Simplifying and Streamlining Your Life

Lightening the Load

- Renewal and Regeneration Through Exercise
- Fuel for Thought
- Banking on Your Future
- Getting a Good Night's Sleep

Base Camp Training

Week 5. Simplifying and Streamlining Your Life

In the fifth week you'll start freeing up time and energy by becoming more focused, organized, and efficient. You'll learn to stop feeling overwhelmed, rushed, or scattered — and start to take control. Think of this as your own personal spring cleaning week.

Week 6. Letting Go and Lightening Up

This is a week to cleanse toxic emotions from your body and mind. You'll learn to shed anger and resentments that consume energy and weigh you down. Daily activities and exercises promote acceptance, forgiveness, and release of unhealthy emotions.

Week 7. High-Power Energetics

This week is about being nourished by three types of love: divine love, love for yourself, and love for others. Love is the most powerful force in the universe. It dissolves fears, quiets troublesome thoughts, and provides inner security. The activities and exercises this week are designed to stir love in you, so that you bring that energy to your Quest for clarity and inspiration.

PART 3. REACHING THE SUMMIT

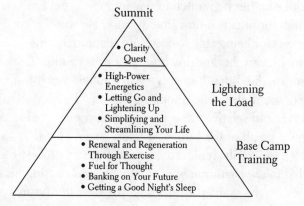

Summit
- Clarity Quest
- High-Power Energetics
- Letting Go and Lightening Up
- Simplifying and Streamlining Your Life

Lightening the Load

- Renewal and Regeneration Through Exercise
- Fuel for Thought
- Banking on Your Future
- Getting a Good Night's Sleep

Base Camp Training

Week 8. Clarity Quest: The Guided Week-Long Sabbatical

This is a week-long getaway to a beautiful setting that will focus you on getting clear answers to questions about your life and livelihood. With the renewed energy and strength you've gained in the previous seven weeks, you can think creatively about the future. You'll emerge with a clear vision of what you want from your life and what steps you need to take to realize that vision.

WHY IT WORKS

Clarity Quest's power comes not only from renewal and restoration but from the *focus* and *structure* that it provides during this time of rest and relaxation. Simply taking "time out" doesn't guarantee that you'll get clear about anything or return with a new vision and plan.

My friend Jim worked for a telecommunications company in Silicon Valley. He was stressed out, burned out, and desperately in need of some time away from his job to heal a bleeding ulcer. His boss helped him juggle his schedule and cut back on projects so that he could take the entire month of December off and think about whether he wanted to stay in the job, cut back on responsibilities, or pursue a new line of work. He was the envy of his co-workers for being able to carve out that much time.

In January he and his boss sat down to discuss his decision. Jim explained that he really hadn't gotten much thinking done. He'd spent the time shopping for the holidays, visiting with friends and relatives, and playing with a new computer—catching up on all of the things he hadn't been able to do before. He had temporarily removed himself from his job stress but had failed to use that time to explore what was causing his ulcer, decide how he wanted to manage stress in the future, or explore his professional options.

Another friend, Amy, was laid off but received a generous severance package. She'd always wanted to change careers and considered this her grand opportunity to spend time thinking about what to do with her life. Amy spent the first month relaxing, taking long lunches, and going shopping with friends. The second month she panicked. She started calling headhunters and sending out résumés to find work in exactly the same field that she'd just left. Without a structured way to examine her options, she was overwhelmed by the fear of making a change.

When I worked in the corporate world, I often fantasized about taking an extended vacation—at least two to four months off with pay. I pictured myself relaxing on a white sandy beach and sipping an exotic drink without a care in the world. I just knew I'd come back relaxed, refreshed, and tan—and would know exactly what I wanted to do with the rest of my life.

My next-door neighbor got my wish. Susan received a large divorce settlement and planned a two-month vacation abroad, hoping it would give her time to unwind, relax, and think through the lessons of her failed marriage and use these lessons to start over. But after three days of sunbathing on the Riviera, she got antsy. Fears about the future started creeping into her thoughts and kept her from relaxing. For the remainder of the trip, she kept busy every waking moment — visiting museums, cathedrals, landmarks, and famous restaurants in all the major cities. She kept her mind totally occupied. When she wasn't touring the sites, she was reading up on them. She came home exhausted and anxious about her future.

Answers come to us when we're rested and quiet. But most of us need some structure and guidance to help us reach that state. The Clarity Quest program gives you that direction and guidance.

The activities included are designed to help free you from disquieting or oppressive thoughts and emotions and to generate feelings of peace, tranquillity, and quiet. *Clarity Insights* will help you release creative blockages and open up the powers of your subconscious mind.

Innately we know what we want. But we spend years of suppressing those desires because of family, personal, and societal pressures. I have a friend who has spent years doing everything "right" — she got great grades in high school, went to a terrific college, landed a stellar job, received annual raises, and married a lovely husband. She woke up one morning, looked in the mirror, and asked, "Who am I really?" and "What do I really want to do?" Throughout the Clarity Quest program, you'll work to access this intuitive knowledge by untapping those inner feelings, dreams, and desires. You'll learn to be more receptive to messages that come to you in the form of ideas, feelings, and dreams — and you'll learn how to interpret and use those insights. Connecting with your deepest desires will help you clarify what you want and show you how to get it.

You've probably heard the expression "Be careful what you ask for, because you just might get it." Well, know now that if you're clear about what you want, commit to get it, and believe that you deserve it — then you *can and will* get whatever you want.

So, put aside all of the "can'ts" and "shouldn'ts" and "oh, it's not appropriate for me." Stop and listen to what you really want.

The minute you clearly define what you want, your mind goes to work to help you get it. How many people do you know who from an early age knew what they wanted and got it? It just requires a little planning and some work. The mind is a broadcast and receiving station. As you become alert to new opportunities, you'll naturally be drawn to people, ideas, and events that will help you get what you want. All sorts of interesting coincidences and unexpected opportunities begin to happen.

RECHARGING YOUR BATTERIES

Each week, this program includes four key activities to renew your energy:

1. Being in beautiful natural settings
2. Enjoying natural light and fresh air
3. Being in peaceful, silent places away from people and man-made noises
4. Taking time-outs

All these activities use the healing and restorative powers of nature, beauty, and silence — and will help you become more attuned to your own intuitive wisdom.

Being in Beautiful Natural Settings

Natural settings absorb our negative energy and fill us up with positive energy. Most of us feel more vital and alive when we're walking on a beach, sitting near a waterfall, walking in the woods, or enjoying whatever beautiful natural setting is close to where we live.

The growing field of ecopsychology studies the powerful connection between nature and mental well-being. Many people experience a heightened awareness in nature; their senses are sharpened; they feel connected to something greater than themselves, more in touch with their own intuitive powers.

My husband, Karl, and I planned a backpacking trip to Lassen Volcanic National Park in northern California following a very difficult live-TV broadcast that I was producing. I had to be "on" for two days, dealing with clients and pumping up nervous and unprepared panelists. When the program was over, an enormous feeling of fatigue came over me. I felt as though I'd held my breath the entire two hours we were on the air. I was exhausted as we set out on the four-hour drive to Lassen, and being cooped up in a car depleted even more of my energy.

I was frazzled by the time we reached the park—but the moment I stepped out of the car, I felt renewed. It was September, but pockets of snow dotted the mountains. Everything was green and lush, and the snowcapped peaks were gorgeous. In the twenty minutes it took to get to our campsite, I felt restored. After setting up camp, I was ready for a five-mile hike. The trail descended right next to a waterfall, and we could feel the spray as we wound our way down. I stayed up until the wee hours of the morning marveling at all the stars and appreciating the glory of this beautiful spot.

You don't have to escape to the country to find natural settings or beauty. Many people in large cities enjoy the calm and tranquillity of parks, botanical gardens, reflection ponds, or the lush green foliage in the lobby of a hotel or office complex. Others find relief from the anxieties of everyday life by listening to the sounds of running water in a fountain or river.

Beauty breaks of all kinds are renewing, and you'll be scheduling them into your weekly activities. A simple trip to a flower shop, museum, art gallery, or card shop can transform a frenzied state of mind into serenity. When we allow ourselves to feel beauty, to let it permeate our souls, we feel more at peace with ourselves and in harmony with the world. Let yourself marvel at whatever you find beautiful—a painting, a person, a tree—and remember that beauty is in the eye, or the soul, of the beholder.

You'll become very familiar with beautiful settings near your home during this program, and you may even discover some new delights. I've found a couple of parks near my house and make stops during my walks to observe the flowers, the moss on a tree, or even a blade of grass. I listen to the sounds in nature and feel the warm rays from the sun on my skin.

Try this experiment. Find a noisy location in the middle of the city, sit there for fifteen minutes, and record how you feel. Then find a beautiful, quiet spot. Sit there for fifteen minutes and ask yourself how you feel.

Enjoying Natural Light and Fresh Air

Research shows that our mood improves when we experience direct, natural sunlight. People who stay indoors all winter and receive only small doses of natural light can become depressed or moody. Sunlight also provides important vitamins for health and well-being.

When we were sick as children, my mother would bundle us up and make us sit outside in the sun for a half hour—even in winter and even though we lived in Montana! The temperature didn't matter. If the sun was out, we'd be outside soaking it up. I would just close my eyes and let the rays penetrate my body. Our illnesses would often disappear within a day.

The fresher the air, the better our oxygen supply. Oxygen is one of the most important nutrients and helps our bodies run efficiently. A few years ago I worked in a newly renovated office complex in Silicon Valley. The windows were sealed shut, and people routinely closed the blinds to prevent glare on the computer screens. There was no natural light, only fluorescence. Almost all of my co-workers experienced frequent headaches, and someone was always sick. In the absence of fresh air or natural light, colds and flu spread like a wildfire in the office. I had to work in that complex only two days a week, but on the days I was there, I often had headaches and my energy level was very low. For me the stagnant air was like a pond with no flowing water, where harmful bacteria could take over.

In this program you'll schedule breaks to go outside. This is especially important if you work in an environment that has low natural light and recycled air.

Don't despair if you live and work in a large city. Janet works in a large high-rise building in Chicago and discovered a wonderful deli that she can walk to during her lunch break. She walks down a beautiful street lined with trees and flowers and in warm weather eats her lunch outside by a fountain. She finds her lunch break to be a welcome relief from office stress and politics. Scout out places to walk to during your lunch break or try walking a scenic way to work.

Being in Peaceful, Silent Places Away from People and Man-made Noises

Silence and solitude help us to see and hear ourselves and others more clearly. A woman attending a workshop recalled an evening she spent while backpacking high up in the mountains next to a crystal-clear lake. After dinner she left her husband at the campsite and ventured down to the water alone to enjoy the wonderful silence that comes only with solitude. The moon was just coming up over the trees and was reflected on the still, calm lake. She sensed the peace penetrating her soul, and she felt at one with nature and with the world. When we're alone and silent, we start to hear the sounds in nature and our own inner wisdom. Some people call it connecting with our higher self.

In nature a certain stillness and silence permeate the early morning right before sunrise and the early evening just after sunset. Being outside at these times can be magical. All living things vibrate with energy. When we're silent and alone, we become part of that peaceful, energizing vibration.

My friend Carolyn shared another kind of experience with silence. She went to a workshop where the speaker asked everyone to be quiet for ten minutes and to look into the eyes of the other people in the room. After that ten minutes of silence, they all had to stand up and give an impromptu speech. Carolyn said that the silence had allowed her to see and hear herself and to connect with other people more deeply. The result was that she gave a powerful impromptu talk. And life is instant improvisation.

During the Clarity Quest program, you'll be asked to take a Silence and Solitude break each week. In a quiet place you'll practice silence for twenty minutes. If possible, try to avoid all man-made sounds, such as cars, construction noises, boom-box music, and people talking. Libraries, museums, parks, cathedrals, and temples are good retreats.

Taking Time-outs

A getaway to a different environment, even if it's only a mental getaway, can do wonders for the soul. Just being in a new place can take your mind off problems, lift you above the fog, and help you think more clearly. Temporarily removing yourself from a situation or simply taking time out to relax and recharge can free your mind and generate enough energy for you to come up with solutions — much as athletes take time out in a game to rest and plot strategy.

When Sandra was in the midst of personal and financial upheavals, one particular weekend getaway was a lifesaver. She didn't have much money, and a getaway seemed like a huge extravagance, but she needed to escape her environment and the persistent problems that seemed to surround her. Every Sunday she scoured the travel section of the newspaper for good deals within a two-hundred-mile radius of her house. Finally she found a motel on the coast that had a great getaway special package. That same week she received a check in the mail for her birthday. Her parents typically sent presents, but that year they sent a check! She called immediately and made reservations, knowing that she could live frugally during her weekend away by making sandwiches for lunch and dinner.

When we're under stress, our most primal urges put us into a "fight or flight" mode. This getaway was her first solo flight. She'd never traveled alone before, and she felt both trepidation and excitement as she started out on the three-hour drive to the motel. She took the most scenic route possible and listened to beautiful soul-soothing music as she drove. It was a spectacular day, and she arrived about 2 P.M. Instead of checking into the motel right away, she took an exhilarating hike along the ocean—exploring beautiful blue tide pools, wandering aimlessly in the fresh ocean air, sitting on rocks, watching birds, and writing in her journal. When it got dark, she checked into the motel and went to her room. She lit candles, had dinner, read an inspirational book, turned in early, and listened to calming music before dozing off.

The next morning she got a cup of coffee and began walking again. She watched the sunrise and gazed out at the ocean in the early morning stillness, feeling peace in her soul as she enjoyed the beginning of a new day.

That weekend she escaped her normal environment and routines. She soaked in the beauty around her and tried not to think about her problems. The book she was reading helped to distract her mind, and so did the beautiful setting and the long walks by the sea. As she walked, she took frequent breaks to record her insights and observations. She was able to quiet her mind and turn down the incessant chatter. By the end of the weekend, she had enough energy to think through her problems. In this beautiful setting they didn't seem as ominous and all-consuming. By the end of the weekend, she'd come up with an action plan. What had seemed impossible before now seemed quite possible.

Getting off the treadmill and temporarily removing ourselves from normal stresses helps us take a long, hard look at what is depleting our energy and what we want to do about it. We can assess more easily what we need to change and look clearly at what we want for the future.

Pay attention to what activities, people, and places help to restore your energy. Some people enjoy listening to music, watching logs burn in a fireplace, or taking walks in the evening. Other people enjoy a drive in the country, the vitality of a busy café, or the stimulation of an intense workout.

HOW TO GET THE MOST OUT OF THE PROGRAM

These seven guidelines will help you get the most out of Clarity Quest:

1. *Be committed.* Commitment is a key to accomplishing anything in life. Halfhearted efforts bring halfhearted results. If you truly want to start feeling better and have mental clarity, stick with the program. When you reserve time on your calendar, commit to keeping that date with yourself.

You have to read only one new chapter each week and work on one week's activities at a time. Focus only on what is before you. When I first started training for a marathon, twenty-six miles seemed an impossible distance to run—especially since I felt out of breath and tired after jogging only two miles. But then I got involved in a program that concentrated on only one week of training at a time. That was manageable. Each time I accomplished the goal for that one week, I felt confident about going on to the next week. In six months I ran twenty-six miles!

2. *Adapt the program to fit your needs.* Clarity Quest is designed to last for eight weeks, but you may want to personalize it to fit your own needs and schedule. For example, if you'd like to start working on your finances first, that's OK. You may want to spend more time on some chapters than on others. That's fine too, but make

sure you allow enough time to accomplish the objectives set forth in *all* the chapters. Without a calm, rested, healthy body and mind, you'll find it harder to think of creative ideas or solutions. Jane, a nurse in Portland, found it difficult to complete all the exercises one week. Because she found them so valuable, she simply extended that part of her program into the next week.

Whatever order you use, make sure that you incorporate Nature and Beauty breaks and Silence and Solitude breaks. These are intended to help you achieve a calm and clear mind as quickly as possible.

3. *Post a weekly schedule of activities in a place where you will see it frequently.* You'll be scheduling weekly activities every Sunday for the upcoming week. Put this calendar where you will see it often, or keep it with you at all times, so that you don't overschedule and can plan ahead—letting friends and family know when you won't be available, requesting days off from work, and lining up baby-sitters if necessary. The busier you get, the more you need to schedule activities in advance.

4. *Plan to do this program when the weather is optimum in your area.* Being outdoors is a major component of Clarity Quest, so try to schedule your eight weeks when the weather permits you to do that. Some people enjoy the cold, but be prepared. Chris, a marketing research consultant in Manhattan, began the Clarity Quest program in the dead of winter. He discovered a great joy in spending time outdoors and simply "bundled up" and enjoyed many quiet and peaceful days in Central Park. He took a week off and headed south for his getaway.

5. *Be willing to accept your inner guidance.* We all have that "still, small voice" within us that knows the truth about what we want and speaks our deepest wisdom, but we have to be open to hearing it and acting on what it tells us. A good friend of mine searched for years for the right livelihood. A banker by profession,

she took an entire year off work to find herself and her purpose in life. She read dozens of books, listened to tapes, and completed lots of exercises. She even went to two career counselors. I think she knew the type of work that would bring her fulfillment, but she wasn't willing to explore that path because it meant less pay and fewer benefits. The result was that she has spent the last eight years unhappy in her work.

6. *Evaluate your progress and reward yourself for achieving your weekly objectives.* Many people begin programs and never see them through to completion. Keep the reason why you started this program in the forefront of your thinking: you want to create your best possible life and livelihood. You might want to write it down and refer to it often.

Eight weeks may seem like a long time when you're first getting started. Remember, you have to work on only one chapter a week— and the activities and exercises at the end of each chapter will help you feel more energetic, better about yourself, and more in control. Fill out the weekly progress reports and celebrate the positive changes that are happening in your life. Use this as motivation to continue. Eight weeks will go by quickly. You can do it! Stick with it! And reward yourself each week for your accomplishments.

7. *Have fun.* Your weekly activities and getaways should be fun—and so should your planning for them. Make all your Clarity Quest exercises and activities fun. Put on great music, sip cappuccino, or brew a fresh pot of tea. It takes far less energy to complete any task when you find a way to make it fun.

PLANNING AND PREPARATION

Before you begin, you need to purchase a few items, set up a quiet area in your home, arrange to take a few days off from work, find a Clarity Quest buddy, locate and research parks near your home, and let friends and family know what your schedule will be for the next eight weeks.

Step 1. Go Shopping

Shopping Items

Blank notebook or sketch pad
Notebook binder with removable paper
Pen (try to find a beautiful pen that's easy to write with)
Marker/highlighter pen
Files
Large calendar to hang on the wall and a portable calendar
Healthy foods for the week
Aromatic bath oils and a natural sponge
Candles

Notice that you need to purchase two notebooks for this program. One should be a binder notebook with removable paper, and the other a bound notebook or sketch pad. The binder will be used to complete exercises that can be tossed away, so make sure that the paper is removable. Important insights, exercises, dreams, and observations that you'll want to remember should be recorded in your bound notebook or sketch pad. Use your marker pen to highlight all inner messages. Consider using a different colored pen to record important lessons learned. During your getaway you'll spend time reviewing your journal, looking for recurring themes and insights. This notebook will become the actual blueprint for your new career and the new life that you create.

Your notebook should be small enough to carry with you to the office, on the bus, in a park, in a library. You never know when you'll get an inspiring idea. I also like to use a beautiful writing tool and often choose calligraphy pens so I can write with a flair! Putting your thoughts, ideas, and plans down on paper helps focus your mind and chart the course of your future.

The foods you buy for this week should be healthy ones. No double-fudge Twinkies this week. We'll talk about the importance of nutrition and energy foods in Chapter 4, but throughout the program you should follow this simple guideline: Eat as many fresh foods as you can, and cut back on caffeine, alcohol, sugar, fat, and salt.

I've suggested purchasing aromatic bath oils and candles to enhance the relaxing ritual of a bath. Don't panic, guys. You don't need to light candles or take a bubble bath to enjoy a relaxing soak or activity. You might enjoy relaxing in a hot tub, sauna, or steam room or listening to music. The key is to remove yourself from your day-to-day pressures and do something that promotes a calm state of mind and body.

Step 2. Set the Stage

Find a special area in your home for your Clarity Quest activities, a quiet space that feels nurturing and inspires creativity. It should be a place where you can relax, dream, and recharge your batteries. You can furnish it with beautiful pictures, brightly colored fabrics or linens, candles, and incense. You might want to keep a basket nearby for favorite quotations, inspirational articles, and poetry.

Janet had a hard time finding a place for solitude in her house. She had roommates and was constantly being interrupted, but she was determined to create a special space and eventually set up an area in her garage. She purchased a space heater and a small carpet. She stacked her favorite books alongside a coffee table and put some favorite photographs and postcards from faraway places in a wicker basket. She found that her mind became expansive when she went to her special place and sat looking at the pictures.

Clarity Quest spaces do not have to be indoors. I have several outdoor places that soothe me. One is a picnic table on a hillside under a beautiful oak tree in a quiet park near my home. I take cassettes there and listen to meditative music or just listen to the music of nature. Sometimes I simply look at the sky and watch the beautiful clouds float by. I can relax and daydream, write in my journal, or work on my blueprint for the future. In the wintertime I love to be in front of a roaring fire. I put on soft music, brew a cup of tea, and bring out my books, journals, and treasured mementos. The key is to create an environment where you can relax and where your mind can wander and explore, a place where you feel totally at ease and at peace in your heart.

Make a ritual of setting up your area. Take time to create the mood. This is a message to your mind that you're putting all your worries aside for a while and moving from anxiety into a calm, peaceful state of mind.

You can even create this space mentally. Some people prefer to go to a place that exists only in their imagination. To do this, close your eyes and envision a beautiful place in nature, a temple, or a church. Look around and see what it's like. Are you sitting next to a babbling brook in the mountains? Are there wildflowers? Animals? What do you smell? Soak in the beauty and majesty. Are you in a small chapel? What does it look like? What does it smell like? Are there candles burning? Incense? Is there an altar? You can go to this imaginary place whenever you want to recharge.

Step 3. Let Important People in Your Life Know What You Are Doing

Be sure to tell friends and family what's involved in your Clarity Quest and carve out enough time for yourself to feel that you've gotten "away." Let them know you'll need some quiet time, some time alone over the next eight weeks. Ask for their understanding and support as you refocus and work on new solutions. Pull out a calendar and share it with your friends and loved ones. If you feel "selfish," remember that this is your time to relax and gain clarity. In the long term it can benefit your family and friends almost as much as it does you.

If you have small children, consider sending them to a relative or friend for certain blocks of time or getting a sitter for your activities and getaway. Try bartering baby-sitting time with a mate or good friend. Some parents get up at 5 A.M. to squeeze in a little quiet time alone before family obligations begin.

Make sure to clear with your boss your time off for the getaway well in advance.

Step 4. Designate a Clarity Quest Buddy

The Clarity Quest process often goes faster when you have someone with whom to talk things over. Find a buddy who is all ears.

One summer when I was ending a relationship, I found a friend who was a wonderful listener. We called it the Summer of Our Discontent. We took long walks together, sharing our stories and our feelings. It was a great comfort just to talk and be heard, and I discovered that when someone really listened to what I said, it was easier to talk through problems and find my own solutions.

If you don't have a friend who can be a Clarity Quest buddy, perhaps you can make this arrangement with a professional counselor, support group, member of the clergy, family member, or spiritual leader. Libraries and coffee shops often have free community publications that list various support groups.

I've also found great value in talking to my colleagues. Sometimes colleagues can relate better to your particular job situation and can even give specific tips or suggestions.

Step 5. Research Local, Regional, and State Parks

To find beautiful, quiet, healing places, investigate the parks and trails in your area. If you don't know where they are, check in a bookstore or look in the Yellow Pages under City Parks, Regional Parks, State Department of Recreation, National Park Service, or U.S. Forest Service.

Find out when the parks are open and what the terrain is like. Discover places that have walking or hiking trails where you can get away from man-made noises. If possible, order maps that give clear directions to the trailheads. Most maps and books indicate the level of hiking difficulty, type of trail, available facilities, and whether or not camping and pets are allowed.

Check with rangers or local officials about the safety and climate of various areas. Ask about animal dangers, plant dangers, and human dangers. Keep an eye out for poison ivy, poison oak, and rattlesnakes—and dress appropriately if it's tick season. Be prepared for heat and cold and sun with lots of sunscreen, water, and layered clothing.

Knowledge is power. During this program you certainly don't want to add one more worry to your list.

Step 6. Begin Research for Your Getaway

Your personal Clarity Quest getaway will take some planning. Begin now to look for hotels, motels, inns, retreats, spas, or campgrounds. It's important to find a place where you can totally remove yourself from your day-to-day distractions. Some people retreat to nature and enjoy the quiet and solitude and beauty. Others find cities to be energizing and restorative and have taken their journals and exercises with them to museums, cafés, and city parks. Start looking in newspapers and travel magazines or call a travel agent. Magazines like the American Automobile Association's *Via* and *Sunset* advertise great weekend getaways. Many spiritual retreats are listed in New Age publications. Some places even let you pay only what you can afford. Begin researching now and set up your own personal file on getaway possibilities.

READY, SET, ACTION

Now it's time to take action. There are a number of preparation and planning activities that you'll need to do before you begin Clarity Quest. It's best to complete these one week prior to beginning the program. You'll begin Clarity Quest on a Sunday, reading Chapter 2, "Week 1: Getting a Good Night's Sleep," and scheduling your activities for the first week of your Clarity Quest. Throughout the program you'll begin most days with a shower, a daily washing-away ritual of anything that could keep you from your greatest health, wisdom, and happiness.

Connie, a communications officer for the Highway Patrol, was feeling very overwhelmed when she first started the Clarity Quest program. She'd heard rumors that her department might be eliminated within the year. Rather than spend the year worrying, she decided to be proactive and take control of her life. Her goal was to use Clarity Quest to think clearly about what she would do if she lost her job. The only problem was her schedule. She worked rotating shifts that changed weekly. She wasn't confident that she could schedule and complete all the activities and exercises each week.

To get beyond the state of feeling overwhelmed, she had to keep focusing on her goal and quickly found ways to fit the activities and exercises into her weekly routine.

CLARITY INSIGHT #1

Your thoughts create your reality.

All thoughts are energy and have the power to manifest into physical form. What we think about determines what we become because that is where we send our energy. We can learn to focus and direct our thoughts and thus create what we want. Improve your thoughts and you can improve your world.

AN EXERCISE TO FOCUS AND DIRECT YOUR THOUGHTS

Find a quiet place. Take a few deep breaths. Pay attention to your thoughts. Are you thinking about a project that needs to be done? Perhaps a call that you need to make or an errand that you need to run? Gently call back your thoughts and energy. Every time you dwell on something negative, you give it power.

Think about what you'd like to accomplish with this program. What do you really want? Who do you want to become?

Imagine a door in front of you. Step through the door and enter the new life that you want to create. What are you doing? What do you look like? How do you feel? What new qualities do you have? Are you respected, self-assured, competent, successful, compassionate, poised, and calm? Make the image as real as possible.

Spend time each day thinking about the positive changes you'd like in your life. You can accomplish whatever you think is possible. To think something into existence successfully, make sure that you want it, commit to get it, and believe that you deserve it. Thoughts mixed with intense feelings such as joy, passion, excitement, and enthusiasm bring about changes more rapidly.

PREPARATION ACTIVITIES AND EXERCISES

- Set up the Clarity Quest area in your home.
- Designate a Clarity Quest buddy.
- Buy stationery and bath supplies.
- Buy healthy foods for the week and try to cut back on caffeine, alcohol, sugar, fat, and salt.
- Locate beautiful hiking trails near your home.
- Block out time for your getaway on your calendar.
- Make a checklist of everything you'll have to do to take the week off for your Clarity Quest (e.g., inform your boss and spouse, line up sitters, arrange for mail pickup).

- ↗ Let friends and family know about your getaway and time needed for exercises and activities.
- ↗ Begin research for your getaway. Set up file.
- ↗ Complete your Progress Report.

PROGRESS REPORT

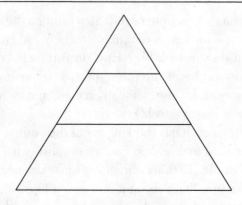

- Think about your goals. What do you want to achieve? What do you want to get out of this program? Complete Clarity Insight #1.
- What would you like to get clear about?
- Is there anything that's holding you back?
- How are you currently feeling? Mentally? Physically? Emotionally? Spiritually?
- What would you like to accomplish this week?

Record your answers in your journal. Include your hopes, dreams, and trepidations.

Part One

BASE CAMP TRAINING

Chapter 2

Week 1: Getting a Good Night's Sleep

▤ *The phone was ringing loudly and persistently as I entered the house after a noonday run. Karl was recovering from knee surgery, and I'd taken a few days off to be with him.*

"Hello," I answered, short of breath.

The caller whispered back, "I'm not supposed to be calling you, but I thought you should know that they're going to close down our operation." It was Kris, one of my colleagues at work. She'd just gotten back from a staff meeting at which the announcement had been made. Closing down our operation probably meant that several people would be losing their jobs, including me. I felt as if someone had punched me in the stomach.

My boss called later in the afternoon to make the news official. She tried to sweeten the blow by saying that not everyone would be losing their jobs and that we wouldn't know for another two weeks who was in and who was out.

I was afraid I wouldn't sleep that night, so I took a couple of over-the-counter sleeping aids before going to bed. I tossed and turned, and my mind continued to race out of control. What would happen to Randall and Ken and Tracey? What would happen to me? I kept

looking at the clock every hour. The sleeping aids weren't working.
Finally, at 3 A.M., I got out of bed and went downstairs.

There was a full moon, and the living room was bathed in its
light. I went around touching everything. It wasn't a bad dream.
I hadn't imagined the phone calls. This was real. My friends and
I would be losing our jobs soon. Life was about to change dra-
matically. I knew that I wouldn't be getting much sleep for many
nights to come.

— JOURNAL ENTRY

If you're worried about your job or contemplating life changes,
you may already have spent a few sleepless nights. You're not
alone. Health officials now report that about half of all American
adults don't get enough sleep to function properly. That's an
alarming number.

Lack of sleep weakens our concentration and impairs our decision making and creative thinking. It also causes health problems
and undermines our immune system. Losing even one night's
sleep can result in anxiety, irritability, difficulty concentrating,
and absentmindedness.

It's ironic that during the exact times when we need to be most
alert and performing at our best, we're often unable to do so because we aren't sleeping well. My friend Todd worked for a company that decided to close down its West Coast operation. As a
result, several positions were eliminated. The company called it a
"rebalancing program," and the "excessed" employees were given
eight weeks to find another job within the company or to resign
voluntarily and get a severance package.

They offered "excessed" employees three classes to help them
in their job search. At the first of these, "Behavioral Interviewing,"
Todd was shocked by his co-workers' appearance. They were
skilled and talented people, but they looked like zombies. They
had dark circles and bags under their eyes, their skin was pallid,
and worry lines were etched across their foreheads. Many had a
distant, faraway look in their eyes. These characteristics are typi-

cal of people who are under a great deal of stress and aren't sleeping well.

Todd noticed that many of these people seemed unfocused in class and often had to ask the instructor to repeat what she had said. He worried that many of them wouldn't be able to find another job. They could hardly concentrate long enough to write a résumé, let alone make a good first impression on an interview. At precisely the time when they needed to put their best foot forward and appear poised, confident, and alert, they were feeling tired, looking haggard, and struggling just to stay awake.

The good news is that you can recover from some of the damaging effects of stress with a good night's sleep. During sleep your metabolism slows down enough for your body to restore itself and for psychological healing to take place. You can recharge your entire system and restore yourself mentally, physically, and emotionally.

Not everyone needs the same amount of sleep to feel rested and restored. Some people can get by with as little as four hours a night, while others need up to ten hours a night. If you tend to sleep in on the weekends, you may be someone who needs more sleep. One way to find out how many hours you need is to note how many hours you sleep, on average, during a relaxing week-long vacation. After a good night's sleep, you should feel rested, refreshed, and ready to handle whatever challenges come your way.

Learning to relax is one of the best ways to keep stress under control and ensure a night of good, sound sleep. The objective this week is to learn how to relax and get enough rest to restore your vital energy. The energy you begin to restore this week will help you to think more clearly and creatively.

WEEK 1 OBJECTIVE

To Relax and Get Enough Rest to Restore Vital Energy

This week you'll learn:

- ✔ Three techniques for relaxing and controlling stress: deep breathing, muscle relaxation, and meditation
- ✔ How to let go of stress and problems
- ✔ What kinds of food, drink, and ambiance promote good sleep

LEARNING TO RELAX

There are hundreds of ways to relax. My friend Jeff relaxes by listening to classical music. He says the music lets his mind float, so that he can think in different ways. My mother rises early each morning to sip tea and quietly stare out the window. She calls this her "quiet time." Another friend unwinds and relaxes by taking long, luxurious baths. She creates a ceremony by lighting candles around the tub and very slowly stepping into the warm, comforting bathwater. While soaking, she takes deep breaths and mentally relaxes all of her tired, aching muscles. My father relaxes by working on home projects. If he puts all his energy and concentration into the task—building a deck or walkway, for instance—he can lose himself in the work. Other people relax by reading books or participating in or watching sports. My husband, Karl, relaxes by going to football games. He becomes so absorbed in the game that he stops thinking about his job or personal worries.

While all forms of relaxation can be beneficial, these three techniques are particularly helpful for controlling stress and promoting health and well-being:

- *Breathing deeply* can help to get you into a calm, relaxed state.

- *Muscle relaxation* helps to release body tensions and frees up blocked energy.
- *Meditation* quiets the mind, helps to focus your thoughts, and draws forward those resources you need to solve whatever problem is at hand.

Deep breathing, muscle relaxation, and meditation all help to reduce anxiety and produce a lasting sense of calm and well-being.

Many types of relaxation provide diversion from day-to-day stress, but not all have a positive effect on your long-term health and well-being. Sometimes the stress or anxiety return the minute you stop doing them. Drinking is a good example. For a while you may completely forget your worries, but the moment you start to sober up, the fears, anxieties, and tensions return, perhaps even more strongly than before.

BREATHING DEEPLY

Have you ever noticed that when you're feeling anxious, you tend to take very short and shallow breaths? It's hard to think clearly, and you feel pressured and rushed.

When you deepen your breathing, you begin to release tension. Taking slow, deep breaths helps to slow your brain waves to an alpha state. Alpha waves typically appear when you are relaxed, during the first stage of the sleep cycle, or when you're sitting or lying quietly with your eyes closed. When you slow down and deepen your breathing, you feel calm and your thoughts become more clear and focused.

You can practice the following breathing exercises anytime you feel anxious or tense, but this week try practicing an exercise in the morning, midday, and evening and record how you feel. Your goal is to slow down your breathing and take deep abdominal breaths. To begin, find a comfortable position, either sitting or lying, and try to breathe through your nose.

Breathing Exercise #1

1. Inhale slowly to the count of 5. Exhale slowly to the count of 5.
2. Repeat 10 times.

Breathing Exercise #2: Slow, Deep, Abdominal Breaths

1. Inhale slowly to the count of 5. Hold your breath and count to 5. Exhale in a long, slow sigh. Pause for a count of 5 before your next breath.
2. Repeat 10 to 20 times.

RELAXING YOUR BODY

Body workers, massage professionals, trainers, and chiropractors say that they can actually feel the excess tension that we hold in our muscles. This tension can block or waste our energy. Try the following exercise to release tension and relax the body.

Muscle Relaxation Exercise #1

1. Sit or lie in a comfortable position. Make sure that your spine is straight. Breathe deeply and take slow, deep, abdominal breaths. Concentrate on each breath.
2. Feel your whole body relaxing, letting go of any problems or tensions.
3. Begin by relaxing the muscles in your feet. Let your toes relax, and release any tension that is held there. Next, think about the bottoms of your feet and your ankles. Slowly release the tension from this area. Imagine your feet becoming loose and limp.
4. Move up to your calves. Work through all the tension that is stored there and let it release down and out through your feet.

5. Next, move up to your thighs and knees. Imagine all the tension being slowly swept down through your calves and out through your feet. Feel yourself getting lighter.

6. Visualize your abdomen and stomach. Relax all your muscles and internal organs. Imagine any tension there moving down through your legs and out of your body.

7. Move up to your chest. Feel the air flowing in and out of your lungs. Let the tension go.

8. Feel the relaxation flowing into your shoulders. Feel your shoulder muscles relaxing, and imagine the tension being swept down through your body.

9. Think of any tension in your arms being released and swept down through your hands. Feel your hands and fingers relax. Release all the tension that is held there, and let it float out through your hands.

10. Allow relaxation to rise into your neck and head. Imagine a broom sweeping the tension away.

11. Go back through your body, and again sweep away any tension that might remain.

12. Feel your whole body relaxing.

13. Continue breathing slowly. Feel lighter and relaxed. Open your eyes.

Muscle Relaxation Exercise #2

Using the above exercise, tighten your muscles before releasing and relaxing them.

Muscle Relaxation and Visualization Exercise #3

Visualization is using your imagination to create a clear mental picture of your successful results. Many people have used visualization to rid themselves of colds, flu, and even cancer. Athletes are encouraged to visualize every detail of their winning performance before they take the field. Visualization works because the subconscious cannot distinguish between situations that actually occur in physical reality and those that are clearly imagined. The more detailed you can picture a situation and the more intensely you feel it, the more real it becomes.

Several years ago, when I was experiencing some health problems, I tried the following muscle relaxation and visualization exercise. I was utterly amazed at how well it worked!

Using Muscle Relaxation Exercise #1, add the following visualization after Step #2: Imagine a golden ball of light above your head. As you inhale, imagine the light coming into your body. Visualize the light shining brightly and as you relax each part of your body, see the light burning away any harmful diseases or toxins.

MEDITATION

Meditation can release fears and negativity, improve concentration, and help you tap into your deep inner resources. Any meditation that lets you relax your body and quiet your mind can help you achieve a higher awareness and find new sources of energy and creativity.

I first tried meditation in high school, following the techniques outlined in a popular book. I think I actually may have quieted my mind once or twice, but it took a lot of time and effort—and in those days I was into instant gratification. Meditation tapes helped ease me into the practice several years later. The music was so soothing and calming that it took me into another state of mind. Today I'm irritable if I can't begin my day with meditation. It keeps me calm and helps me tap into great inner guidance and direction.

The secret to meditation is *sticking with it*. It takes discipline and perseverance to focus properly. Set aside a certain amount of time each day, and just keep practicing. If your mind starts to wander, gently bring it back. The more disciplined you become, the better your results will be.

You don't have to sit cross-legged for thirty minutes to meditate or to induce relaxation. You can practice by simply sitting comfortably or lying down. People with some experience in meditation can even practice it while walking, sitting at a bus stop, or do-ing other activities like washing the dishes or raking leaves. Every time you relax your body and mind and quiet your mental chat-ter, you gain clarity and focus.

Affirmations, visualizations, imagining a thought or picture in your mind, repeating a word or a phrase, and breath control are all helpful techniques for focusing your energy and keep your mind from wandering.

- *Affirmations* are positive statements of what you want to cre-ate. When you repeat these statements over and over in the present tense, your subconscious mind starts to accept them as true.
- *Repeating a word, beautiful passage, sound, or prayer* over and over can help focus your thoughts and improve concentra-tion.
- *Taking deep, natural breaths* can help you to release tension and become centered. Your thoughts become more vivid and clearly focused.

To begin meditating:

1. Try to meditate at the same time each day. Pick a time when you will be undisturbed for at least 30 minutes.
2. Find a spot that's peaceful and quiet. If you haven't found a peaceful place outside, your quiet Clarity Quest area may be the perfect location.
3. Find a comfortable sitting position, either in a chair or on the floor—or else lie down. Keep your spine straight to allow a good flow of energy.
4. Close your eyes and begin breathing slowly and calmly. Take 10 to 20 slow, deep breaths. Be aware of your breath moving in and out. As you inhale say, "I receive." As you exhale say, "I let go." Let go of any tension or pain in your body. Exhale all the tension until you feel calm and peaceful.

5. Relax your body. Using the muscle relaxation technique, mentally go through your body and relax each part. Imagine a flame of white light going through your body, removing all impurities and tensions.
6. Imagine roots at the bottom of your feet. As you continue breathing slowly, imagine the roots going down deep into the earth.
7. Focus on an object, an affirmation, a passage, a prayer, or a word. Repeat it over and over. If any thoughts come into your head, imagine sweeping them away.
8. When you feel calm and relaxed and are ready, open your eyes. Take a few moments to slowly reorient yourself. Take a few deep breaths and stretch.

When you are in a calm and peaceful state of mind, you conserve energy. That energy can be used for engaging in productive activities, coming up with creative solutions to problems, or climbing to new heights.

You can practice the breathing and muscle relaxation techniques throughout the day, but try to make meditation a habit by doing it at the same time each day. Many people like to meditate first thing in the morning so that they begin the day in a calm and relaxed state. This week you might want to try meditating both in the morning and in the evening just before you go to bed. I like listening to meditation tapes before I drift off to sleep. It helps me feel calm and peaceful, and I go to sleep with a smile on my face.

GUIDELINES FOR GETTING A GOOD NIGHT'S SLEEP

Our habits during the hours just before we go to bed often determine how well we sleep. Allan referred to himself as a technoslave. He carried his beeper and cell phone with him at all times and checked his e-mail right before going to bed each night. His beeper and home fax machine would ring throughout the night, often disrupting his sleep. Before starting Clarity Quest, he had no sacred withdrawal time from his work.

Allan made a wonderful discovery during his first Silence and Solitude break. He left all of his electronics at home and took a long walk in the woods. He returned feeling refreshed and renewed and later decided to shut down all work-related intrusions two hours before going to bed at night. He turned off his beeper, fax machine, and cell phone and wrote down a list of what he would work on first thing in the morning. Allan started sleeping more soundly and discovered he was much more focused and productive during the day.

Here are some suggestions for the hours before bedtime.

Six Hours Before Going to Bed

Stop eating or drinking anything with caffeine in it.

Three Hours Before Going to Bed

Avoid eating, drinking alcohol, and smoking cigarettes. A full stomach can affect the quality of your sleep. Alcohol can relax you and might help you *get* to sleep, but it can also affect the quality of your sleep. Nicotine can act as a stimulant.

Foods with tryptophan have been known to promote sleep. Some foods that contain tryptophan include turkey, milk, dry-roasted soybeans, sunflower seeds, pumpkin seeds, and baked potatoes with skins. Remember not to eat a lot, however, because your body needs time to digest the food.

Two Hours Before Going to Bed

Stop exercising. A good workout earlier in the day will help you sleep better, but your body needs time to return to its normal resting state before sleep.

Make a list of your problems so that they have a place to be while you sleep and put work aside.

One Hour Before Going to Bed

Read only soothing literature, and listen to and watch only calming programs. There are many troublesome, violent messages in the media that can weigh heavily on your mind during the night. If anything strikes a dissonant chord, don't partake in it right before bedtime. This includes unpleasant conversations. Don't answer your phone an hour before going to bed if you think the caller might overtax your mind or emotions.

Limit how much liquid you consume before going to bed. If you drink too much, you'll probably have to get up during the night— and you might interrupt a wonderful dream. A cup of chamomile tea or a glass of warm milk can help you relax, but try not to drink too much right before bedtime. Some herbs that have been known to promote sleep include hops, passionflower, hawthorn, and valerian root. Be sure to take them in the recommended quantities. Calcium and magnesium, taken in the evening, have also helped some people relax.

Take a warm bath.

Make sure that your room is comfortable and quiet. The temperature shouldn't be too hot or too cold, and your bed should invite peaceful slumber. Try to go to bed at the same time each night.

Thirty Minutes Before Going to Bed

Try meditating or listening to quiet, soothing music. Imagine yourself drifting off to a calm and peaceful sleep. Sweet dreams!

CLARITY INSIGHT #2

*Your dreams can help you reach a deeper
understanding of yourself.*

Dreams are a doorway to the unconscious. They bring messages
from the deepest part of us. Our dreams can help us get in touch
with the world beyond our physical reality and help us tap into a
great reservoir of knowledge and wisdom. By learning how to listen to and interpret our dreams, we can reach a deeper understanding of who we are and what we can become.

START RECORDING AND
INTERPRETING YOUR DREAMS

1. State your intention to start taking your dreams seriously.
   Be open to receiving dream messages and acting on them.
2. Before going to bed, state out loud, "I will remember my
   dreams," and repeat it at least ten times. Pray or ask for
   dreams that will give you clear guidance.
3. Keep your journal and a pen next to your bed. Write down
   your dreams immediately upon wakening. Most dreams
   are forgotten within minutes of waking.
4. If something about your dream is not clear, ask yourself
   what the dream meant. What can it teach you? Pay attention to images and symbols. Try to understand what
   each symbol is telling you. Suggest to your mind that
   greater understanding will come to you. Be aware of messages that come from people, books, advertisements, and
   other sources as well. Talk about your dream with a
   friend. Look for clues. You might not understand a
   dream right away, so record all messages in your journal
   with a special colored pen—or highlight them.

5. Pay attention to recurring dreams and messages. Important messages usually repeat themselves.
6. If you're looking for a solution to a problem, ask for it in your dreams. Affirm to yourself before going to sleep that your dream will provide you with an answer.

Learning to understand your dreams may take a while—just as developing and strengthening a muscle takes time. If you want more guidance, look for books on dreams in the bookstore or library.

WEEK 1 ACTIVITIES AND EXERCISES

Review the guidelines for getting a good night's sleep. Keep your journal and a pen near your bed so that you can record your dreams. Remember to take a cleansing shower each morning.

Sunday

- Take an early-morning shower. Focus on the water gently washing away any fears, blockages, attitudes, thoughts, or feelings that are holding you back. Imagine them washing down the drain, and emerge feeling cleansed and refreshed.
- Take a Silence and Solitude break. Find a quiet, peaceful location and spend at least 20 minutes there alone. Be still and listen to the sounds around you.
- Review your calendar and map out activities for the week.
- Set up your bed and bedroom to ensure peaceful sleep.
- Select peaceful, soothing music for the week or purchase a meditation tape.

Monday

- Meditate 20 to 30 minutes.
- Take a midday break. Find a peaceful, quiet location, preferably outdoors, and practice a breathing exercise.

- Take a warm bath, listen to soothing music, or meditate before going to bed.

Tuesday

- Meditate 20 to 30 minutes.
- Practice a muscle relaxation exercise.
- Before of after dinner, take a beautiful 30- to 40-minute evening walk. Breathe slowly and observe all things of beauty.

Wednesday

- Meditate 20 to 30 minutes.
- Take a midday break. Find a peaceful, quiet location, preferably outdoors, and practice a breathing exercise.
- Take a warm bath, listen to soothing music, or meditate before going to bed.

Thursday

- Meditate 20 to 30 minutes.
- Take a Beauty break. Enjoy a trip to a museum, card shop, art gallery, flower shop, or park. Marvel at what you find beautiful and record how you feel.

Friday

- Meditate 20 to 30 minutes.
- Practice a muscle relaxation exercise.
- Take a warm bath, listen to soothing music, or meditate before going to bed.

Saturday

- Take a walk with your Clarity Quest buddy.
- Complete your Progress Report and reward yourself for completing the activities this week!

PROGRESS REPORT

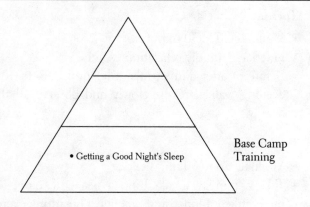

Base Camp
Training

• Getting a Good Night's Sleep

- What did you accomplish this week?
- Do you feel more rested and relaxed?
- Record your feelings and insights in your journal.

Record your answers in your journal. Include your hopes, dreams, and trepidations.

Chapter 3

Week 2: Banking on Your Future

⚏ *I feel such relief! I finally took pencil to paper today and worked out my finances. It was a grueling exercise, but by the end of the day I felt so much more in control and much less fearful. Fear is a funny thing. It stalks silently, ready to attack when I'm feeling low and weak. I've been so fearful about money for such a long time. Over and over, I've debated whether I could leave my job and survive or had to stay, unhappy but continuing to receive a paycheck. Just thinking about it would make my heart start to race, and a wave of panic would come over me.*

Today I took charge. I took a long, hard look at the next six months of my finances. I reviewed the worst-case scenario and best-case scenario—and discovered that I actually could survive without a job for six months! I wouldn't have to rush into anything. I'd have some time to get focused, time to think before I leapt. My fears began to dissipate. I felt back in control.

— JOURNAL ENTRY

Money. It prevents so many people from pursuing their dreams. It's the first thing people think about when facing a life change, like a divorce, a job layoff, or the possibility of taking some time off work. It's most people's number-one fear and greatest source of stress.

Money fears take an inordinate amount of energy—and Clarity Quest is about conserving energy for deeper thinking and more creative ideas.

The objective this week is to free yourself from monetary worries by simply compiling a personal financial plan and learning to use physical and verbal affirmations for abundance. Having a plan on paper and consciously tracking your expenses helps you *get in control* and minimizes unnecessary worry. It also helps identify surplus funds that can be used to build a career safety net or plan a getaway to jump-start a new life.

WEEK 2 OBJECTIVE

To Free Yourself from Monetary Worries

This week you'll learn:

- ✔ How to gain financial peace of mind
- ✔ How to use physical and verbal affirmations for abundance

DEVELOPING A PLAN FOR PEACE OF MIND

John worked in the same department at the phone company for sixteen years. He wasn't challenged by his job and often toyed with the idea of taking a leave of absence. The only thing that held him back was fear about money. He kept himself paralyzed for years by going around and round with the same old questions: Do I have enough money to survive without a paycheck? For how long? Will I be able to cover all my monthly expenses? Will I need to dip into my savings? Will I need to find temporary work while I'm taking some time off?

A friend in Los Angeles was also consumed with fears about money. She felt trapped in an unhappy marriage and worried that if she left her husband she wouldn't have enough money to "survive." She jointly owned an expensive house; owed heavy lease payments on a BMW; and all her credit cards were maxed out. She took a job to prepare herself financially for a divorce. It was the wrong move because she acted without real planning. She hated the job and it involved a two-hour commute during rush hour. She was so stressed out by her new job and exhausted from all the driving that she had no energy to think about what she wanted to do with her life —and how to untangle herself from an unhappy marriage.

Financial peace of mind comes from being in control of the money you have and knowing that you can acquire more money when you need it. Many people are so busy with their 101 "to do's" each day that they don't take time to develop a financial plan or track expenses, so they miss the peace of mind that comes from a little thought and planning.

PUTTING TOGETHER YOUR OWN FINANCIAL PLAN

Use your binder notebook to map out your own financial plan. You might want to copy the following two exercises in your journal or on 8½ × 11-inch pieces of paper. Putting numbers down on paper and developing a plan helps you take an objective look at your situation and more accurately decide:

1. How long you can survive on your existing resources
2. If you should cut back on some expenses
3. When you need to supplement your income with part-time work

After completing both of the following worksheets, you should have a bird's-eye view of where your money comes from and where it goes.

A single mother in a workshop was very fearful about money. She routinely spent more than she made each month and kept sinking deeper and deeper in debt. She was terrified to know the truth about how much she owed and was apprehensive about completing the exercises.

I know how frightening it feels to be desperate about money. When I was going through a divorce and struggling to keep my business afloat, I was often strapped for cash. My first priority was to pay the rent each month and then try to juggle the other expenses. There just wasn't enough money to satisfy all my creditors. It was a scary time, and rather than confront my financial situation, I tried to adopt the "ignorance is bliss" attitude. I was only fooling myself. My situation only got worse. Finally my fears no longer let me ignore my finances.

Once I summoned up the courage to take a hard look at my financial situation, I immediately started feeling much more in control. I could quickly assess my situation and identify what changes I needed to make. I discovered that both *knowledge* and *action* are powerful antidotes to fear.

Financial Statement Balance Sheet

This Financial Statement Balance Sheet will determine your assets and liabilities. From that information, you can determine your net worth. Most people discover that their net worth is greater than they imagined and feel good after completing this exercise.

ASSETS		LIABILITIES	
Cash Reserve Assets		Home Mortgage:	_____
Cash on Hand:	_____	Other Mortgage:	_____
Checking Account:	_____	Automobile Loans:	_____
Savings Account(s):	_____	Bank Loans:	_____
Money Market Funds:	_____	Personal Loans:	_____
Certificates of Deposit:	_____	Charge Account Debt:	_____

Debt Repayment:	_____	Taxes:	_____
Severance Check (minus tax withholding):	_____	Other Debts:	_____
Other:	_____		

Property Assets

Home: _____

Other Real Estate: _____

Automobiles: _____

Furniture: _____

Appliances: _____

Art, Jewelry & Other Valuables: _____

Investments

Stocks: _____

Bonds: _____

Mutual Funds: _____

Annuities: _____

Limited Partnerships: _____

Rental Real Estate: _____

Business Interests: _____

Other: _____

TOTAL ASSETS: _____   **TOTAL LIABILITIES:**_____

(Add cash, property, and investments)

To find your net worth, subtract your total liabilities from your total assets.

TOTAL ASSETS   _____
– TOTAL LIABILITIES   _____
NET WORTH   _____

Monthly Income, Expenses, and Net Cash Flow

This worksheet helps you analyze your cash flow each month. Since income and expenses can vary from month to month, try to estimate your cash flow through all twelve months and then take a twelve-month average. Without looking at the whole year, you might forget to add items like quarterly taxes or annual license fees. Also remember to put your getaway expenses (including gas, lodging, and meals) into the budget.

Any surplus funds can be put into a special "safety net" account. A good rule for most career explorers is to have enough money set aside to meet at least six months of expenses. This is especially necessary for people who want to explore a completely different career track.

MONTHLY INCOME

Wages, Salary, Tips: _____

Unemployment: _____

Alimony, Child Support: _____

Dividends from Stocks, Mutual Funds, Etc.: _____

Interest on Savings and Checking Accounts: _____

Social Security: _____

Benefits: _____

Pensions: _____

Other Income: _____

TOTAL MONTHLY INCOME: _____

MONTHLY EXPENSES

Mortgage Payment or Rent: _____

Other Mortgages (2nd home, vacation): _____

Automobile Loan: _____

Credit Cards: _____ *

Federal Income Taxes: _____

State Income Taxes: _____

FICA & Medical: _____

IRA or Keogh: _____

Savings: _____

Real Estate Taxes: _____

Other Taxes: _____

Utilities (Electricity, Heat, Water, Telephone): _____

Household Repairs & Maintenance: _____ *

Food: _____ *

Clothing: _____ *

Education Expenses: _____

Child Care: _____

Automobile Expenses (Gas, Repairs, License): _____ *

Other Transportation: _____ *

Life Insurance: _____

Homeowners Insurance: _____

Automobile Insurance: _____

Medical, Dental, Disability Insurance: _____

Unreimbursed Medical, Dental Expenses: _____

Entertainment, Dining: _____ *

Recreation, Traveling: _____ *

Club Dues: _____

Clarity Quest Getaway: _____

Newspapers/Magazines: _____

Other: _____

TOTAL MONTHLY EXPENSES: $_____

Total Monthly Income: $_____

Total Monthly Expenses: −$_____

SURPLUS Income: $_____

(Subtract expenses from income)

---

*These expenses are dangerous. They are areas in which it's easy to overspend and not really know how much you've spent until your bank or credit card statement arrives at the end of the month.

HOW IT WORKS

Let's look at an example of how to use this form. If you have money already set aside or plan to receive a severance check or a divorce cash property settlement, you can determine how many months you can survive on that money by dividing your total surplus income by the amount of money you'll need to pay your expenses each month.

Let's say you've just lost your job and received a $15,000 severance check. You'd like to live on this money while you explore alternative careers. This will be your only source of monthly income. After completing the monthly expense exercise, you find that you need $2,625 a month just to meet expenses. Before you deposit your check and consider it income, find out if taxes are withheld and if the withholdings are adequate. Most companies withhold taxes, but it's wise to check with appropriate tax authorities to make sure that you won't encounter an unpleasant surprise later on. For the purposes of our example, let's deduct 30 percent for taxes. Obviously the taxes and expenses will vary from state to state. Here's how that worksheet would look:

MONTHLY EXPENSES

Mortgage Payment or Rent:	$1,200
Other Mortgages (2nd home, vacation):	_____
Automobile Loan:	_____
Credit Cards:	$ 50*
Federal Income Taxes:	_____
State Income Taxes:	_____
FICA & Medical:	_____
IRA or Keogh:	$100
Savings:	$ 50
Real Estate Taxes:	_____
Other Taxes:	_____

Utilities (Electricity, Heat, Water, Telephone):	$100
Household Repairs & Maintenance:	_____ *
Food:	$350*
Clothing:	_____ *
Education Expenses:	_____
Child Care:	_____
Automobile Expenses (Gas, Repairs, License):	$50*
Other Transportation:	_____ *
Life Insurance:	_____
Homeowners Insurance:	$30
Automobile Insurance:	$70
Medical, Dental, Disability Insurance:	$100
Unreimbursed Medical, Dental Expenses:	_____
Entertainment, Dining:	$200*
Recreation, Traveling:	_____ *
Club Dues:	_____
Clarity Quest Getaway:	$325
Newspapers/Magazines:	_____
Other:	_____
TOTAL MONTHLY EXPENSES:	$2,625
Income	$15,000
Minus Taxes (30%)	− $ 4,500
Total Income	$10,500

*These expenses are dangerous. They are areas in which it's easy to overspend and not really know how much you've spent until your bank or credit card statement arrives at the end of the month.

Divide $10,500 by monthly expenses of $2,625 to discover that on your $15,000 severance check, with no other source of income, you could survive for four months without lowering any expenses—and have money set aside for your Clarity Quest getaway.

TIPS TO STRETCH YOUR MONEY

Here are three tips for getting the most from your money:

1. *Let your money work for you.* If you're lucky enough to have an initial surplus fund, investigate putting your money into a savings account, money market fund, or interest-earning checking account. Shop around for the highest rates and best withdrawal policies. You'll feel better knowing that your money is working for you. Pay yourself from this account only what you need to live on each month.

2. *Keep a weekly log of all expenses.* Separate your monthly expenses into two areas: expenses that you pay with a check and expenses that you pay with cash, credit card, or ATM card. Try to pay as much as you can by check. It's one of the easiest ways to keep track of what you spend. You can also carry around a small notebook and write down the amount each time you buy something. Tally your totals at the end of each week.

Many expenses vary from month to month, and these can often be trimmed. For example, you can take public transportation instead of paying for gas, tolls, and parking. You can shop in factory outlet stores or wait until items go on sale.

3. *Pay yourself a lump sum of cash weekly.* A great way to make sure that you don't overspend is to add up all of the starred items in your budget and pay yourself that amount of cash weekly to handle those expenses. Buy all of your necessary items like food and gas first, and when the money runs out, don't pay yourself additional funds until the next week. I remember falling in love with a sweater that cost $60. I only had $20 in cash left after buying my groceries and filling my car up with gas. I wanted that sweater but was determined not to use a credit card. I simply asked the sales-

clerk if I could put it on layaway and agreed to pay $20 weekly. In three weeks I owned a beautiful $60 sweater.

ACQUIRING MORE MONEY

If you find that you need more money, you can do one of four things:

1. *Look for part-time work to supplement your income.* Many part-time jobs don't drain much energy or distract you from thinking about what you'd really like to do. Sometimes doing a completely different kind of work sparks creativity, and taking action to keep up with expenses almost always helps calm fears. I've known some people who kept acquiring debt month after month because they didn't want to waste their energy on work that they considered menial or not in their chosen field. The debt just kept growing, and so did their worries. Before long, the worries consumed more energy than a part-time job would have.

Some good part-time work possibilities are construction work, sales, waiter/waitress, telemarketing, clerical, or even walking dogs, house-sitting, or being an extra in the movies. A former bank vice president in Marin County, California, was without a job and signed up with a casting agency to be an extra in the movies. He loved it and paid his mortgage for an entire year with part-time acting. He also had free time for job hunting and networking.

Another friend hired on temporarily as a construction worker. He was fifty years old and had been a white-collar professional his entire working life when he started working side by side with eighteen- to twenty-year-olds. He was tired at the end of each day, but he found his dream job within six months and learned two very valuable lessons:

a. Doing something "constructive" helped calm the fears that had almost paralyzed him when he first lost his job.

b. Doing physical work that required a different kind of "mind" power helped him get into a relaxed state in which he could think rationally about his next career move.

I've known people who cleaned houses ($45 per house) while making a transition and daydreamed about their futures while they vacuumed. The key is to take part-time work that does not use up all your energy.

2. *Cut back on expenses.* A friend in Chicago took the first full-time job she was offered because she was so fearful about money. It was a job very similar to the one she'd quit—a job she'd hated. She probably wouldn't have been so desperate to take the first job offered to her if she'd been able to scale back her expenses. Since she was renting an apartment and leasing a car, she had some choices. She could move to a more modest apartment or consider renting out one of her rooms. (If you are considering moving, remember to consider all the additional costs: first and last months' rent, security deposits, renting a truck or hiring a moving company, and so on.) She could have leased an economy car, taken public transportation, or carpooled. She could have cut back on dining out, rented movies instead of going to theaters, and invited friends over for potluck.

At the end of each week, look at your expense log and see if there are some items that you can scale back, shop around for, or eliminate entirely. Betsy and her husband loved to dine out twice a week. She liked getting out of the house, sampling new foods, people watching, and having quality time alone with her husband. They usually spent about $50 per dinner. After her husband, David, quit his job, they considered eliminating dining out entirely to save $400 a month—but rejected the idea because it was such a pleasant experience for them and so good for their relationship. Instead, they chose inexpensive restaurants, dining at one restaurant each week, and pretending they were food critics. They had a lot of fun and still saved $150 a month.

Two other couples saved on baby-sitters by taking each other's children on alternate Saturday nights. One couple would baby-sit all the kids the first Saturday night, and their friends would watch the kids the next Saturday night.

Brenda loved to cook and entertain. She invited friends over once a month for dinner but discovered just how expensive entertaining was after tracking her expenses for a month. Her solution was to have each friend bring a different course. Everyone had fun, and she saved $100 per party.

3. *Tap into savings or other assets.* Ideally, you should have six months' salary set aside in your savings account for a job loss or emergency, but the few people who are actually prudent enough to do this are often the most reluctant to dip into their savings. Keep in mind that a job hiatus is usually temporary. If you do need to use your savings or other assets to help meet monthly expenses, work out a plan to pay back the amount you borrow from yourself.

4. *Add debt or borrow money.* This is obviously the least desirable way to acquire money. Payments on borrowed money only increase your monthly expense total. The borrowed funds eventually run out, and you're left with higher monthly payments. I've known several people who have taken out a second mortgage on their homes and found that it was very hard to keep up with their increased payments.

It's tempting, but dangerous, to use your credit cards to float cash. Interest rates on credit card money are so high that it's easy to go deeply into debt very quickly. A friend did this while she was waiting for a government contract to come through. It was a fairly large contract, and she assumed she'd be able to repay her credit card debt immediately. But ironing out the details of the contract took longer than she'd expected, and the interest on the money she borrowed outpaced her ability to pay it back.

If you can't pay your bills, let your creditors know that you are in a temporary financial bind. They will usually let you work out a lower monthly payment. You can also use the services of non-profit consumer credit counseling services. Rather than feeling desperate about money and letting your worries consume all your thoughts, get help by calling the National Foundation Consumer Credit line at 1-800-388-2227.

ABUNDANCE AND SCARCITY

There are two ways to think about money. You can think that the world is plentiful and filled with a great abundance of resources and money, or you can think that life is full of shortages and scarcity.

Scarcity Thinkers

Two types of behavior reinforce scarcity thinking—being a spend-thrift and being a miser.

A spendthrift wants to buy everything now, because he believes that at some point the money will run out and it's better to spend it all now before it's gone. My colleague Bob's severance package included a full year's salary, profit-sharing, and retirement bene-fits—quite a large sum. He quickly made a grand sweep of every store in San Francisco, buying the finest European cotton shirts, three pairs of Gucci loafers, and a beautiful Coach leather brief-case—not to mention enough T-shirts and socks to last for five years. He was like a squirrel gathering nuts for the winter. Stock-ing up brought him great pleasure.

Needless to say, his money ran out quickly, and he'd spent most of it before he'd investigated his tax obligations. At tax time he owed the government a great deal of money and his nest egg was nearly gone. He had to dip into his profit-sharing money and suf-fered severe tax penalties for withdrawing funds early.

A miser is the complete opposite of a spendthrift, but he is still a scarcity thinker. A miser tries to stretch every penny. Janet wor-ried about losing her job and decided to scale back—so far back that she was barely living. She ate a frugal diet of rice and beans, disconnected her cable, stayed home, and didn't go out with friends for fear of spending money. She became isolated and lonely, like a plant that shrivels up when it isn't watered.

Ultimately, scarcity thinking produces scarcity, but it can be difficult to avoid being a scarcity thinker when no money is coming in. Being out of work is a scary time. When you let your fears take over, you may assume the worst will happen—you'll starve, you'll be homeless. These thoughts are irrational, but some people start to believe that the tide will be at low ebb forever. The natural flow of life shows us that tough times won't last forever if you don't let them.

Abundance Thinkers

People who believe the world is a place filled with scarcity allow scarcity into their lives. People who believe that the world is filled with abundance allow abundance into their lives.

Any form of success is first created in our minds. Physical and verbal affirmations can be powerful statements to the mind that the world is an abundant and prosperous place and that we deserve financial peace of mind and success.

Our subconscious minds store messages that affect our behavior. We all know people who were told when they were children, "You're so stupid" or "You'll never amount to much," and some part of them believed and acted on those statements. The subconscious mind accepts what we tell it over and over again. Unfortunately, much of what we tell it is negative. If we change that self talk to positive statements, our subconscious begins to believe those new messages and acts on them. We start to achieve our goals and become more successful. By verbally or physically affirming the good we want, we begin to bring about that good.

VERBAL AFFIRMATIONS

Verbal affirmations are positive statements that help focus the mind on creating what we want. To create affirmations, think of the good you'd like in your life and the personal qualities that would bring that good into physical reality. Make your statements as simple as possible and always state them in the present tense. That way, your mind will work to make them happen more quickly. Say "I am abundant" rather than "I am going to be abundant." Affirmations should be repeated at least ten times a day.

Jeff used the following affirmations when he was experiencing money problems. When he first started to say these affirmations, he owed $3,400 on an old beat-up Honda and wanted to pay off $5,000 of credit card debt. He was amazed to discover the power of verbal affirmations and paid off both debts within six months.

Money flows into my life.
I am prosperous.
I use my money to create good in my life and other people's lives.
I deserve abundance.
I am in control of my finances.

Write down your own verbal affirmations and practice saying them aloud ten times a day.

PHYSICAL AFFIRMATIONS

Physical affirmations are deeds that we do to remind ourselves that we are deserving. We make a statement to our subconscious that we believe in ourselves and that we deserve to be treated well by others. This is especially important during times when our self-esteem may be low and our ego deflated.

During transition times you may not feel you can spend much money—and you may be right. A new Lexus might make you feel great at first, but the worry and lack of self-esteem that follow when you can't make the payments might be devastating.

There are ways to feel abundant and special and to treat ourselves well without spending a lot of money. We can do simple, inexpensive things that give us pleasure and make a statement to our subconscious that we believe in abundance. The more we remind ourselves that we're special, the more that we unfold and blossom. Especially if you're not getting positive strokes from people around you, give positive strokes to yourself. And give strokes to others. You can't help feeling special when you're making someone else feel special.

Make a list of physical affirmations that bring you pleasure and make you feel abundant. Your list should include items that are within your budget. When I was going through my divorce, I included a category in my budget called Special Times Money. This was the cash that remained after paying all the necessary weekly expenses. I could spend it any way I wanted and often used it for physical affirmations. It amazed me how many life-affirming actions required no money at all! Here's my list. I've divided it into two categories: things that make you feel good and cost no money, and things that make you feel good and cost under $25.

Things That Make You Feel Good and Cost No Money

Take a long walk in a beautiful area.
Camp out in the backyard and watch the stars at night.
Watch the sunset.
Sleep in on the weekend.
Nap in the afternoon.
Visit an old person in a convalescent home.
Dress up and go window-shopping.
Put on foul-weather gear and go for a walk in the rain.
Attend a free lecture.

Spend an afternoon in a beautiful park.

Read a best-selling book (borrow from a friend or check out at the library).

Write a letter to a loved one.

Spend a day at the beach.

Go bike riding.

Visit local churches.

Get makeup done for free in a department store.

Visit local Toastmaster clubs (great speeches, great entertainment).

Read old love letters and journals—and make a list of what you've learned.

Get together with a supportive friend.

Check the newspaper for local events, free lectures, and "free days" at art museums.

Make a list of all the people who love you and provide unconditional love.

Listen to favorite CDs, tapes, or records.

Lie on the grass and watch the clouds.

Stay up all night and watch the sun come up.

Visit all local parks in your area, and visit your favorite haunts regularly.

Go for a run.

Check out new books or movies at the library.

Things That Make You Feel Good and Cost Less Than $25

Buy a luxurious bubble bath, light candles, and take a hot bath.

Buy a new paperback novel or magazine.

Buy a new cologne or aftershave.

Buy a hardcover novel in the discount section of a bookstore.

Attend symphony, ballet, theater, or opera matinees.

Rent a canoe and go canoeing.

Purchase a subscription to a favorite magazine.

Buy silk underwear.

Buy beautiful greeting cards and send one to a friend.

Check out designer clothes at department stores, then try to find them at a discount store, factory outlet, or consignment store (make this a fun Saturday outing; include a relaxing lunch or tea time).

Rent in-line skates.

Buy new makeup.

Buy a new tie.

Get a new haircut.

Read *The New York Times*, sipping an iced mocha at an outdoor café.

Go to any local museum.

Cook something new for dinner.

Paint with watercolors.

Buy classical music tapes or a foreign language tape.

Sign up for a local community college class.

Buy beautiful stationery and write a letter.

Listen to beautiful music, light candles, create a mood.

Go to a sporting event. For kicks, go to a high school game and be glad that you're older.

Get a massage (some massage schools offer a full massage for only $20).

Splurge and buy decent champagne at a wholesale or discount store.

Make a picnic and invite a friend to watch the sunset.

Check out local recreation department classes in tennis, watercolor painting, or sailing.

Buy your favorite foods (especially comfort foods from childhood).

Have an all-night movie marathon: rent your favorites and watch with friends.

Jeremy, a marketing manager for a consumer goods company, wants to quit his job and go into business for himself. Unfortunately, he is still paying off graduate school loans and fears that he'll have to continue working in the corporate world for several more years. By analyzing his cash flow and brainstorming ways to make more money, he was able to put together a plan to pay back his loans quickly. He advertised for a roommate and took a part-time job.

Compiling his plan helped to free up valuable energy that he intends to use to do some serious thinking during his Clarity Quest getaway. He's excited about defining the type of business that he wants to start and mapping out a plan to make it a reality.

CLARITY INSIGHT #3

Doubts, fears, and limiting beliefs
block creativity and clear thinking.

You can open yourself up to new opportunities and possibilities by letting go of doubts, fears, and beliefs that are no longer useful to you. When you do that, your energy flows more easily to the new things that you want in your life, and you can make rapid changes. Use the following exercise to release thoughts, beliefs, and feelings that could prevent you from reaching your goals. Repeat this exercise as often as necessary. Doubts, fears, and limiting beliefs block energy. Each time you remove a blockage, you become more clear about what you want.

EXERCISE TO RELEASE FEARS, DOUBTS, AND LIMITING BELIEFS

Find a quiet place. Close your eyes and practice your breathing. Take slow, deep breaths. Imagine each breath filling your body with light. Imagine each exhalation removing any blockages. Open your eyes. Answer the following questions and record your answers.

- Is there any person, emotion, or belief that's preventing you from reaching your goal? Think about where your energy is blocked.
- What are your fears? What's the worst possible thing that could happen?
- Do you believe that you deserve to get what you want?
- Think about your life in 5 years, in 10 years, and at the end of your life. If you don't work to remove these blockages and never achieve your goals, how will you feel? Close your eyes and feel the emotion.
- Now imagine that you've reached your goals. How do you feel? Is your life more meaningful? Are you making a greater contribution to society?
- Write down ways that you can mentally, physically, and spiritually remove these blockages. Imagine yourself living a joyful, happy, and fulfilling life.

WEEK 2 ACTIVITIES AND EXERCISES

Remember to take a cleansing shower each morning. Wash away all fears, blockages, attitudes, thoughts, and feelings that prevent you from having a healthy and fulfilling life.

Sunday

- Take a Silence and Solitude break. Find a quiet, peaceful location and spend at least 20 minutes there alone. Be still and observe the sights around you.
- Complete Clarity Insight #3.
- Review your calendar and map out activities for the week.

Monday

- Meditate 20 to 30 minutes.
- Take a midday break. Find a peaceful, quiet location, preferably outdoors, and practice a breathing exercise.
- Prepare Monthly Income and Expense Worksheet.

Tuesday

- Brainstorm 10 ways to make more money. Record in your journal.
- Prepare Financial Statement Balance Sheet.

Wednesday

- Meditate 20 to 30 minutes.
- Before or after dinner take a beautiful 30- to 40-minute evening walk. Breathe slowly and observe all things of beauty.

Thursday

- Brainstorm 10 more ways to make money. Record in your journal.
- Look over the Physical Affirmation list. Create your own list of physical affirmations. Spend some time in one of your favorite places and write down everything that makes you feel special. Choose one activity and plan for Saturday. For the remainder of the program, try to select one item each week and do it.
- Create two or three verbal affirmations. Think abundance! Repeat 10 times daily.

Friday

- Meditate 20 to 30 minutes.
- Take a Beauty break.

Saturday

- Take an early-morning walk with your Clarity Quest buddy.
- Complete your Progress Report.
- Reward yourself for completing the activities this week.
- Enjoy your physical affirmation!

PROGRESS REPORT

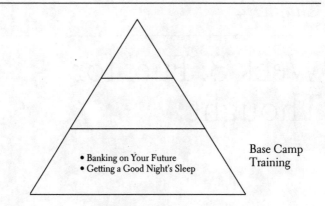

Base Camp
Training

- Banking on Your Future
- Getting a Good Night's Sleep

- What did you accomplish this week?
- Do you feel more in control of your finances?
- Do you feel more relaxed? More energetic?

Record your feelings and insights in your journal.

Chapter 4

Week 3: Fuel for Thought

We had unusually heavy rains during the winter, and the soil was leached of nutrients. In the spring I planted healthy vegetable starts. In less than a month they'd all turned a sickly pale green color and the leaves were plagued by insects. I was horrified. What was happening to my beautiful garden? I picked a few leaves and took them back to the nursery for a diagnosis.

The plant expert explained that the plants were severely undernourished. The vegetables were under stress, and without a heavy dose of fertilizer they would die. In their weakened state they attracted not only diseases but also harmful insects. I learned that a healthy plant is resistant to many harmful diseases and insects. An unhealthy plant becomes an attractive host.

— JOURNAL ENTRY

We human beings are like those unhealthy plants when we are under stress and undernourished. Our immune system is weakened, and we are susceptible to a number of diseases. Sometimes we even draw unhealthy people to us and let them affect our well-being.

During challenging times we need even more nourishment to replenish what stress has destroyed. I am convinced that it's just as important to nourish our minds and souls as it is to feed our bodies healthy food.

Growth, vitality, and health all depend on the quality of fuel we give our bodies and our minds. This fuel is our energy source and directly affects how we feel and perform. The objective this week is to learn how to fuel the body and mind for optimum health, vitality, and energy. If you're getting adequate sleep but still feeling fatigued, lethargic, or irritable, you may not be providing your system with the right type of fuel.

WEEK 3 OBJECTIVE

To Fuel the Body and Mind for Optimum
Health, Vitality, and Energy

This week you'll learn:

- ✔ How to design a personal nutrition plan that helps combat the negative effects of stress and gives you more energy
- ✔ How to satisfy your senses and visualize an energetic, healthy body and mind
- ✔ How particular foods, activities, people, and information affect your energy

BODY FUEL

What goes into your mouth directly affects your health and energy. When you eat healthy, wholesome foods, you feel healthy. When you eat foods that are rich in fat, salt, and sugar, you feel sluggish and lack energy. Good nutrition is the fuel and foundation of mental and physical performance.

A couple of times a year my friend Jan goes on a cleansing program to rid her body of toxins and reassess her nutritional needs.

She fasts on fruit juices for a couple of days and then slowly starts to refuel her body with healthy, nutritious foods. She cuts out caffeine, alcohol, processed foods, fried foods, and added sugars and salts. She feels wonderful. She experiences a surge of energy. Her body feels like it is running efficiently, and her thoughts seem to flow more freely as well.

Information on diet, nutrition, and health is easy to find these days. The secret is to discover a nutrition plan that works for you, one that fits your lifestyle and leaves you feeling energetic. Crash diets and quick-loss eating plans can help you lose weight quickly, but after the first week or two you may start to feel terrible and realize that your body simply isn't getting enough fuel for vitality and health.

I gained thirty pounds during my first year in college. I would literally eat full bags of M&Ms, cookies, and potato chips in one sitting. I was nervous and insecure, and eating was one of the few things that comforted me. I tried to eat away my doubts and fears about my classes and new environment.

When I returned home for the summer, I was appalled at how I looked in a bathing suit. My thighs had taken on a life of their own. I was upset that I couldn't fit into many of my clothes and wanted to lose the weight immediately. In fact, it took more than five years to lose the weight permanently, and during those five years I tried every popular crash diet. One diet had me nibbling pineapple throughout the day. Another had me loading up on bacon and pouring heavy cream into my coffee. I took diuretics and bought cases of liquid protein diet drinks. I lost ten pounds pretty quickly on all the diets, but I felt physically and psychologically deprived. After about two weeks of practicing great discipline, I would always break the diet and start to binge again. My poor body was out of balance and starved of nutrients.

Then, during a vacation to Europe, I made an important discovery. I decided to take a vacation from dieting as well, and I actually lost weight! I was so excited about exploring and sightseeing that I would eat only when I was hungry, and only foods that I craved. I found that eating more complex carbohydrates kept me full for hours at a time. I found that eating just a little piece of chocolate and savoring every bite satisfied my sweet tooth. I didn't eat out of boredom, stress, or fear. I was too excited about other things and found that listening to my body—really listening—helped me eat only what I actually needed. I walked many miles each day, which also helped keep my weight in balance and my body running efficiently. I was amazed at my discovery. Eating more carbohydrates and less sugar and fat kept me feeling full and satisfied—and I felt more energetic than I had in years.

Once I stopped focusing on my weight, I started focusing on a healthy and energetic body. I've held that vision in my mind and haven't been on a diet for more than fifteen years. I discovered a simple eating plan that's easy to remember and works!

THE BASICS

The three basic elements of a healthy nutritional program are:

1. Know thyself—and listen to thy body.
2. Satisfy your senses.
3. Visualize an energetic, healthy body.

Let's look at them one at a time:

Know Thyself—And Listen to Thy Body

The first maxim inscribed on the temple at Delphi is "Know thyself." This is also the first lesson in understanding how to fuel your body properly.

Experiment with this idea: Try different food combinations, and don't worry about calories. Instead, think about proper fuel. Release yourself from all the stress associated with trying to lose weight. Just release it and listen to your body.

Without this stress and guilt, I've found very few people who want or need to eat compulsively. If you eat out of boredom, find other creative outlets. Learn a new skill, meet a new friend, or walk a new path. If you eat to compensate for emotional discomfort, take time to investigate what emotional needs aren't being met. Find the foods that give you sustained energy. Eliminate foods that make you feel sluggish and tired.

When you start fueling your body with proper nutrients, you'll have the energy you need to explore many alternatives and options. It's your body, and you owe it to yourself to find the best possible fuel.

If you listen, your body will tell you exactly what fuel and nutrients it needs.

Satisfy Your Senses

Practice enjoying and savoring your food. Buy the freshest produce available, and take the time to prepare it in a way that enhances its flavor. Relish the taste.

Karl and I often go to a neighborhood Italian restaurant where the food is always excellent. The meats and poultry are among the best I've ever had in my life. I asked Roberto, the owner, what his secret was. "It's simple," he said. "I buy the freshest and finest quality of meats, poultry, and produce available. To prepare a great dish, you have to have the best and freshest ingredients." It makes sense. Not only do fresh foods taste exquisite, but they also have more vitamins and minerals than frozen or processed meals.

I believe that when we eat quality foods, and when we really taste and savor every bite, we forget about quantity. We only keep eating and eating when we're not satisfied and have stopped listening to our bodies. Mediocre food that isn't fresh or tasty does not satisfy us. Nor does it give us as many vitamins and minerals. I am reminded of those large buffet-style restaurants. Some of them have started serving more fresh foods, but others still offer people plates full of food that had been sitting in steamers all afternoon. One flavor bleeds into another, and it's difficult to distinguish tastes or textures. When you go to restaurants, try to order fresh foods prepared in a way that enhances the natural flavors.

Take time to enjoy your meal. My client Sheila likes to buy fresh flowers and set a beautiful table. Each night she lights candles and puts on quiet, soothing music. It helps create a relaxing atmosphere and makes the meal more enjoyable.

When I was in high school, my mother encouraged me to take a home economics class because she worried that I wasn't "domestic" enough. Most of the girls in my class (sorry, no guys at the time) concentrated only on the cooking and baking. My team concentrated on presentation. We found a drawer full of beautiful placemats and place settings. As we went around the room and sampled the various dishes, I realized that our food tasted better simply because of how it was presented—even though there may have been a few ingredients missing.

Years later, when I was in the catering business, I rediscovered the value of presentation. Eating involves most of our senses, not just taste. An entree that's visually appealing and aromatic also tastes better and makes the dining experience much more enjoyable.

Visualize an Energetic, Healthy Body

What we manifest in our lives is first created in our thoughts. The better we can picture or feel something, the easier it is to bring it into physical reality. Our friend Steve knows what it feels like to be healthy, so it's very easy for him to recapture this feeling and to visualize himself as healthy. He also knows exactly how he wants to look physically. He holds that picture in mind and never needs a scale to tell when he's a few pounds overweight. He feels it and knows that it doesn't match the picture in his mind. He naturally readjusts his eating habits whenever his physical body doesn't look and feel the way he envisions it.

Another friend of mine attends a weight-loss class weekly. To use her words, she has "struggled with her weight for years." She's not terribly overweight, but I'm not sure that she has a clear picture of what she wants to look or feel like. She doesn't see herself as thin; she sees herself as overweight and struggling with it.

Be careful about what you say to yourself. If you say, "I always struggle with my weight," "I have a hard time losing weight," or "Losing weight is not easy for me," then losing weight will probably be a struggle. Hold a vision in your mind of what it feels like to be healthy and energetic. You might see yourself enjoying life fully and doing all the things you've wanted to do. Sarah likes to visualize a lean and efficient machine. While she's walking or jogging, she chants to herself, "I feel great. I eat healthy wholesome foods. I'm filled with energy, my body runs efficiently, and my mind is clear and focused."

A SIMPLE EATING PLAN

This simple plan is based on the principles we've just discussed. It is designed specifically to give you more energy and to combat the negative effects of stress.

1. *Stop dieting and start listening to your body.* It will tell you what it wants and needs. If you haven't listened to your body for years, it might take a while to get back into communication. Be patient. Think in terms of long-term energy and health. You might want to begin with a cleansing fast of fruit and vegetable juices and water for a few days to free your body of toxins. An eating plan should be tailored to your individual needs. Some people have discovered that they need to eat more proteins and less carbohydrates. Like automobiles, people require different types of fuel and fuel additives to help them run efficiently. If you have health problems, consult with your health care provider.

2. *Vary your foods and eat in moderation.* The key to any successful eating program is to eat well-balanced, nutritious foods in

moderation and to vary them often. If you eat the same foods every day, you may not be getting the full range of nutrients to achieve optimum energy. I used to love to eat toast with peanut butter every morning, a turkey sandwich for lunch, and salad and chicken for dinner. Because I didn't vary my foods, I wasn't getting the right balance of nutrients—and my energy level reflected that deficiency.

3. *Eat more complex carbohydrates.* Complex carbohydrates are the preferred source of energy and should make up the largest part of most diets. They burn slowly and provide a more consistent blood sugar level. Complex carbohydrates can be found in whole grains such as wheat, oats, barley, brown rice; vegetables such as corn, peas, potatoes; whole grain pasta; and dried lentils and beans.

4. *Make sure that you're getting enough fiber in your diet.* Fiber, the nondigestible part of plants, helps our bodies run efficiently by cleansing our intestinal tract and eliminating waste. To add more fiber to your diet, eat more whole grain foods, dried beans, and fruits and vegetables, like raw apples, carrots, broccoli, cabbage, and salads. You can also add a fiber supplement from the health food store, such as unprocessed raw bran or psyllium seed husks.

5. *Eat more fresh fruits and vegetables,* at least four to five servings a day, preferably raw. Valuable vitamins can be lost in cooking. Organically grown foods are free of chemicals and toxins and give you better nutrients.

6. *Drink at least eight glasses of water a day.* Water constitutes over 60 percent of your body weight and keeps every body process functioning, including circulation, digestion, and excretion. If you are concerned about the quality of your drinking water, have it analyzed. You can buy purified, distilled, or spring water or invest in a water filter.

7. *Cut down on fat and animal protein.* Most of us consume much more fat and protein than we need. A high-fat diet can cause heart disease. Most people eat the equivalent of an entire stick of butter every day. To become familiar with how much fat you are consuming, read the labels on packaged foods. Avoid fast foods, fried foods, and saturated fats. Fatigue and poor concentration can be directly linked to a diet high in sugar and fat.

Most people get the majority of their protein from animal and dairy products that are loaded with fat. The majority of your protein should come from poultry, fish, low-fat dairy products, soy products, and dried beans and peas.

8. *Eat less salt, sugar, and processed foods* (canned foods, TV dinners, and anything that is pre-prepared). Sugar is a quick energy booster, but it burns quickly and leaves you feeling fatigued and irritable. Sugar can also make it hard for you to concentrate. It is a common food additive—so again, read the food labels. Almost all packaged and canned foods and processed meats are loaded with salt, preservatives, and artificial additives. Try to avoid foods that are loaded with these additives. The body's efforts to fight the effects of these additives can leave you feeling drained.

9. *For more consistent energy, try eating small meals or snacks more frequently throughout the day.* This will help to keep your blood sugar levels more constant. Don't skip meals.

10. *Cut back on your intake of alcohol and caffeine.* Coffee can increase alertness, but it's also very dehydrating. I love the taste of coffee and, after years of drinking five or six cups a day, struggle with cutting it out of my system completely. I now make a blend of half regular coffee and half water-processed decaf. I limit myself to a few cups in the morning, but I treat myself to the best flavors available. I also love a fine glass of wine, but I know my limits.

If I drink too much, I feel sluggish and groggy in the morning. Alcohol and caffeine dehydrate the body, so for each glass or cup that I consume, I try to drink one glass of water.

11. *Stop smoking.* Smoking, caffeine products, alcohol, sugar, and stress all deplete our bodies of energy.

12. *Take additional supplements* when you know that you're not getting enough nutrients during the day. If we all ate a well-balanced, chemically free diet and lived in a stress-free, pollution-free environment, we'd probably never need to supplement our diets. But I don't know anyone who fits this description. Even my grandmother, who lives in a small town in Montana, suffers the effects of pollution, stress, and food preservatives. There are several herbs and supplements that can help to combat stress and fatigue and enhance mental energy. Consult a nutritionist, health food expert, or your physician to see if you need to supplement your diet and what supplements might help. All added supplements can be dangerous if not taken properly and can actually deplete your energy if taken in doses that are too high or too frequent. This includes food supplements and herbs.

A SIMPLE PLAN TO GET BACK IN BALANCE

Whenever you've had too much to eat or drink, use this simple cleansing program to help restore your energy. The idea is to get the overindulgence out of your body as soon as possible. On the "day after," I suggest the following:

1. *Drink a lot of water and eat a lot of fresh fruits and vegetables.* Both help to flush your body of toxins.
2. *Sweat the poisons out of your body.* Go on a long, strenuous

hike or run. Make sure that you break a sweat. This helps to break up poisons and get them out of your body.

3. *Eat high-fiber foods or take a fiber supplement.* A gentle fiber will help cleanse your colon.

MIND FUEL

Various kinds of foods, activities, information, and people affect your energy in different ways. Pay attention to what drains you and what makes you feel energized. What you digest mentally is just as important as what you feed your body.

If you feel that your energy is being drained, make a list of all of the people, TV shows, books, and newspapers that you suspect are taking your energy rather than raising it. Which people drain you of energy, and which energize you? Do certain kinds of newspaper articles make you depressed or inspired? When you listen to the radio or watch TV, do you feel refreshed and inspired or drained and depressed? Do soap operas and sitcoms refresh you, or do they leave you feeling heavy and sluggish? What about music? Do certain kinds of music lift you up? Do other kinds leave you sluggish or rattled? All these things can uplift us, or they can drag us down. It's almost as if we have a ball and chain attached to our foot. That extra weight depletes our energy, energy that we might instead use to explore new people, places, and things.

Pay attention to your energy levels, especially during this time of renewal and reflection. Judy used to watch the ten o'clock news before going to bed each night. She didn't filter anything out; she just took it all in. On the evenings that she watched the news, she would toss and turn throughout the night and wake up several times. She was restless, not at all in the peaceful state that brings nurturing sleep. When she switched to watching comedy at night instead of the late-night news, she would wake up feeling refreshed and reenergized. She discovered that the news drained her, possibly because her mind kept working on the stories, and that she was better off watching something else.

What she read would affect her in the same way. Depressing stories of rape, murder, and war weighed her down. Inspirational stories had the reverse effect. She felt lighter, more buoyant, and happier.

It's just as important to select what enters our minds as it is to choose the foods we want to eat. The good news is that we have a choice. We can control what we read, watch, and listen to—and we can make sure that information is nutrient-rich information, not junk food. We can cleanse our minds of toxic waste, just as we do our bodies.

Try monitoring what your mind ingests each day. Keep a log of all the information you take in, and write down how it makes you feel. Here is how that log might look.

Information You Digest and How It Makes You Feel

Read

NEWSPAPER
Fearful. Angry. Confused. Hopeless. Apathetic. Grateful. Enthusiastic. Inspired. Joyful. Serene. Hopeful.

COMPUTER ARTICLES
Fearful. Confused. Hopeless. Grateful. Enthusiastic. Serene. Hopeful.

E-MAIL
Happy. Hopeful. Appreciative. Angry. Resentful. Overwhelmed.

BOOKS
Curious. Loving. Excited. Fearful. Withdrawn.

MAGAZINES
Excited. Fearful. Confused. Hopeless. Grateful. Enthusiastic. Inspired.

MAIL
Fearful. Angry. Confused. Hopeless. Apathetic. Grateful. Enthusiastic. Inspired. Joyful. Hopeful.

Listen To

RADIO TALK SHOWS
Angry. Fearful. Confused. Hopeless. Excited. Righteous.

AUDIOTAPES
Serene. Hopeful. Grateful. Enthusiastic. Inspired. Joyful.

FRIENDS
Relaxed. Happy. Angry. Grateful. Enthusiastic. Inspired. Joyful. Hopeful.

CO-WORKERS
Fearful. Angry. Confused. Grateful. Enthusiastic. Joyful. Hopeful.

OTHERS
Angry. Resentful. Apathetic. Joyful. Excited.

Watch

TELEVISION NEWS
Fearful. Angry. Confused. Hopeless. Apathetic. Inspired. Hopeful.

TELEVISION PROGRAMS
Relaxed. Happy. Fearful. Angry. Confused. Joyful. Serene.

MOVIES
Fearful. Angry. Confused. Hopeless. Excited. Inspired.

PEOPLE AND ENERGY

Other people can have an enormous impact on your energy. I have a close friend whom I love dearly. We have used each other as sounding boards for many years. Strangely, I found that when I was facing a job layoff, it was difficult to be around her. She had many challenges of her own that needed attention, and at the time I had a hard time shielding myself from others' problems. I would listen to someone else's problem and find myself wanting to solve it for them.

My being a sounding board for her was a great comfort to her. But my role as a sounding board drained all my energy. I would leave her feeling weighed down and much heavier than I had felt before we got together. My friend wasn't ready to listen to solutions. I discovered that most of the time and energy that I invested in helping her was wasted—and that I didn't get much support in my own challenging situation. I certainly didn't want to abandon my friend during this difficult time, but until I could build stronger boundaries around myself and shield myself from her problems—just listen and not take them on—I needed to avoid seeing her for a while.

In contrast, I found that spending time with another friend during this time invigorated me and lifted my spirits. She wasn't tangled up in her own problems, and luckily, I didn't bring her down. We would spend time examining and discussing various situations in our lives, and then we would explore solutions. The minute we went from dwelling on a problem to exploring solutions, we became invigorated and buoyant.

Think about the people with whom you spend your time. Who drains you of energy, and who recharges you? Start to notice when people are zapping your energy. Friends are treasures in our lives, and I'm not suggesting that you abandon any of them. However, if some people drain you, stay away from them until your own energy is in balance. The emergency instructions in planes tell parents to put on their own oxygen masks first and then help their children. You can't be of much help to others unless you can help yourself first.

Sharon was wary about starting Week #3. She had tried to lose weight for years without success and associated all dietary suggestions with dieting. She joked with friends that the first three letters of the word diet were "die" and that she often felt she was slowly "killing" herself with diets.

Sharon realized that her goal in this program was to fuel her body for optimum performance, not to lose weight or to starve herself to death. She thought about the types of foods that a coach or a guide would recommend if she were training to climb a mountain. Her attitude shifted. She looked forward to planning her meals and made shopping for her "performance fuel" an adventure. She bought lots of fresh vegetables and fruit at a local farmers' market and found wonderful fresh breads, pastas, fish, and chicken at a local health food store. She also purchased yogurt and trail mix for snacks. She decided to give up coffee and alcohol for one week, just to see if it made any difference in how she felt. The first day she had a severe headache due to caffeine withdrawal. It went away by the third day, and she found that she was sleeping more soundly at night and had more energy.

Sharon was committed to this "eating plan" for only one week, but she felt so good by Saturday that she decided to continue eating healthy foods for the remainder of the program.

CLARITY INSIGHT # 4

Listen to your inner messages for guidance and direction.

You can receive wonderful guidance and direction by simply listening within. Begin to pay attention to insights that come to you in the form of ideas, flashes of inspiration, strong intuitive feelings or gut feelings. These are messages that can guide your path and help you make decisions quickly and easily. Take a notebook with you this week to record all inner messages. Sometimes, fearful thinking can interfere with this inner guidance. Review your recorded messages and ask yourself, "Is this valuable guidance or fearful thinking?"

The following exercise will help you get in touch with your inner voice.

AN EXERCISE TO HELP YOU LISTEN
TO YOUR INNER GUIDANCE

Before beginning this exercise, quiet your mind and get centered by meditating for 10 to 20 minutes.

Imagine a mountain before you. Your goal is to reach the summit. You begin your ascent in a beautiful meadow filled with flowers. As you start climbing, you follow a narrow path through a forest. The path follows a stream, and you notice colorful rocks, ferns, and wildflowers. As you wind your way upward, your path narrows. You come to a clearing and see a high mountain lake. The aqua blue water is glistening in the sun. You stop for a while to admire the scenery. You feel energized and excited to continue on your journey.

You walk around the lake and come to a fork in the path. You have a choice to make. Should you take the path to the right or to the left? Each path represents a choice you're considering. In your mind imagine the choices written on a sign in front of you. The sign indicates each path's level of difficulty and how many miles it will take to reach your destination. What do the signs say? Which path does your heart tell you to take? Which choice feels lighter? Listen for messages from your body. What does your gut tell you about this choice? Quickly scan your body. Do you feel a heaviness in any part of your body? What does this suggest to you? Do you foresee any hardships ahead? Imagine setting out on one path and learning that it was the wrong path. What is that path like? Do you eventually turn around and return to the other path? Which path leads you to the summit in the easiest and most joyful way? Does this feel like the right path to take?

WEEK 3 ACTIVITIES AND EXERCISES

Remember to take your notebook with you this week and record all inner messages. Take a cleansing shower each morning.

Sunday

- Take a Silence and Solitude break. Find a quiet, peaceful location and spend at least 20 minutes there alone. Be still and observe the sights around you.
- Complete Clarity Insight #4.
- Review your calendar and map out activities for the week.
- Review the 12-step eating plan and design your own nutrition plan for the week. Plan to cut back on coffee, caffeine drinks, alcohol, sugar, fats, meats, and salt. Buy healthy foods.

Monday

- Take a midday break. Find a quiet location, preferably outdoors. Visualize a healthy body and how it feels to have an abundance of energy.
- Create two or three verbal affirmations. Think healthy, energetic body and mind. Add to your abundance affirmations and repeat 10 times each day.
- Log the people with whom you associated, and what you ate, listened to, and read today. Record in your journal how you felt while you were doing each activity.

Tuesday

- Meditate 20 to 30 minutes.
- Take an evening walk. Practice your breathing exercises and observe all things of beauty.

Wednesday

- Take a Beauty break.
- Log the people with whom you associated, and what you

ate, listened to, and read today. Record in your journal how you felt while you were doing each activity.

Thursday

- Meditate 20 to 30 minutes.
- Take a midday break. Find a quiet location. Visualize a vibrant and healthy body and mind.

Friday

- Practice your muscle relaxation exercises.
- Log the people with whom you associated, and what you ate, listened to, and read today. Record in your journal how you felt while you were doing each activity.

Saturday

- Take an early-morning walk with your Clarity Quest buddy.
- Create your own eating plan and mind-fuel plan for the rest of the program.
- Complete your Progress Report and reward yourself for completing the activities this week.

PROGRESS REPORT

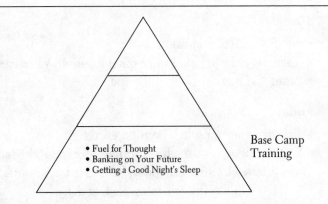

- Fuel for Thought
- Banking on Your Future
- Getting a Good Night's Sleep

Base Camp
Training

- What did you accomplish this week?
- Which foods, activities, information, and people drain your energy? Which energize you?
- Are you willing to eliminate the energy zappers? How?
- How are you feeling?

Record your feelings and insights in your journal.

Chapter 5

Week 4: Renewal and Regeneration Through Exercise

▦ *Slipped out of bed early this morning. I had so many worries on my mind and hoped that an early-morning run would exorcise a few of them. The sun had been up for a while, but it was shining brightly only on the mountain peaks above. The valley remained shaded and cool.*

I started running slowly—a nice jog-walk pace. My muscles were stiff and I felt sluggish. My feet felt heavy as they hit the pavement. To keep my mind off all the little aches and pains, I tried to focus on my breathing. About a quarter of a mile into the run, the sun began to filter through the trees, and my senses became sharper, more aware, more acute. I could smell the early-morning aromas of wet grass, pine trees, wildflowers, and somewhere coffee over a campfire. I began to notice things in greater detail—the moss on the trees, the pine needles, and the blue lupine and tall grass swaying gently in the early-morning breeze.

It felt wonderful to be moving, to feel fluid and in tune with nature. My worries seemed to melt away in the sunlight, and I started to think about possibilities. It felt good to be alive on this glorious day!

—JOURNAL ENTRY

Would you be interested in a medicine that could reduce anxiety, make you more productive, and increase your self-confidence? What if I told you that this same medicine could control body weight, combat stress, provide a defense against diseases, improve posture and appearance, and add more zest and vitality to your life. And what if I said that it was safe and proven effective for almost everyone, regardless of age or gender. Sound too good to be true? It's not. The medicine is exercise—and in a sense, it is a miracle.

While not a cure for all problems, exercise can calm your fears, increase your strength and stamina, and raise your energy level. The objective this week is to start exercising to reduce the harmful effects of stress, think more clearly, and have more energy. You'll learn how to get started, stick to an exercise program, and enjoy the benefits of aerobic exercise.

WEEK 4 OBJECTIVE

To Begin a Program of Exercise That Reduces the
Harmful Effects of Stress and Promotes Clear
Thinking and High Energy

This week you'll learn:

- ✔ How exercise can calm fears, reduce stress, increase energy, and promote well-being
- ✔ How to get started and stick with an exercise program

THE BENEFITS

Exercise has profound benefits that affect every area of our lives:

1. *Physical benefits.* Exercise increases your strength and endurance. It improves cardiovascular health, delivers oxygen and blood more quickly and efficiently, and tones up the muscles.

2. *Mental benefits.* Exercise also delivers more blood and oxygen to your brain. Your mind is stimulated, more aware, and you can think more clearly. You become more imaginative and more creative.

3. *Emotional benefits.* Exercise produces beta endorphins, an opium-like substance that helps your body resist pain and helps you feel better about life and about yourself. Beta endorphins have a tranquilizing effect that helps you feel calm and more positive. Even after you stop exercising, you feel more calm and at peace.

It's hard to pick up any paper or magazine these days without reading about the benefits of exercising. So why is it so difficult for so many people to start and continue an exercise program?

THE CHALLENGES

Almost anything can get in the way of beginning and sticking with a program of exercise. Some of the most common roadblocks are demanding schedules, family obligations, not being in the habit of exercising, not sticking with it long enough to feel the benefits, being bored, not having enough time, and not having role models.

Demanding Schedules and Family Obligations

Frank's story illustrates the problems of demanding schedules that don't leave enough time for exercise. At forty-one, he is a successful businessman who is married and has two daughters. In high school he was captain of the debate team, vice president of his senior class, and had a 3.8 grade-point average. His interests have always been purely academic—never athletic. In college he took a full load of classes each semester and worked part-time in a local deli. He graduated with a degree in electrical engineering, started working right out of college, and at the age of twenty-three married his high school sweetheart. Frank continued to work very hard. By the time he was thirty, he had been promoted three times.

Frank was on a successful career track, and having two young children at home demanded a lot of time and attention. At age thirty-eight, Frank was promoted to vice president. He continued to work evenings and weekends and would simply have a couple of drinks to relax. Exercise had never been a part of Frank's life, and he certainly didn't think he had time to spare for it now.

Not a Habit, Didn't Stick with It, Bored

Nancy is forty-three years old and a public relations manager for a bank. Her company has downsized twice in the last five years. In addition to worrying about her job, Nancy also worries about her weight. She has enrolled in more than a dozen exercise classes over the last four years. She was excited to take each new class, but within a month her enthusiasm would wane. She has taken beginning tennis, beginning aerobics, and beginning step classes.

In the aerobics class Nancy had a hard time following the instructor. She found herself jumping around, trying desperately not to hit the person next to her or make a fool of herself. She discovered in tennis that she had no eye-hand coordination, at least during the first week. She would run around a lot but missed more balls than she hit. It wasn't a fun experience, so she quit after a few weeks. Step classes seemed easy at first. The routines were easy to follow—simple marches and simple up and down steps on a platform in front of her. But when everyone started stepping up and down, then turning around, pivoting, and clapping their hands, she got hopelessly lost. She didn't return a second time.

Weight training was a little different. She learned how to lift the weights and with a trainer established an easy routine. But it was so boring. It didn't take long before she found a lot of other things that demanded her attention, and she stopped going to the gym. Nancy was quite enthusiastic about buying her own exercise equipment. In the privacy of her own home, she could exercise while watching TV or even reading. For about a month she tried exercising at home but soon got bored and found herself only watching television—uninterrupted by exercise.

No Time, No Role Models

Art is twenty-eight years old and works for an advertising agency. He routinely oversleeps in the morning, so it's a mad scramble to catch the bus and make it to work by 9:00. He's a dedicated employee and often works until 8:00 at night. By the time he gets home, he's weary and looks forward to picking up a six-pack of beer and some fast food for dinner. Most evenings are spent eating dinner in front of the TV and falling into bed by midnight. On weekends he likes to sleep in. Sometimes he has his friends over to have a few beers or take in a movie or a game.

Art's friends have similar work demands and lifestyles. When they get together, they talk about their favorite TV shows and lack of a real "life." They are classic couch potatoes.

The excuses for not exercising are varied, and often they seem very valid. It can be hard to squeeze in the time to exercise unless you exercise regularly—and it's hard to get hooked, to see and feel the benefits, unless you do it over a period of time.

I've had some pretty good excuses in my life. I was not athletic in high school or college, and I had a hard time motivating myself to start an exercise program. Intellectually, I knew that exercise would help me feel better about myself, but it was difficult to start moving. When I first began jogging, I lived in San Francisco with my first husband, Joe. Many mornings he practically had to dynamite me out of bed to go jogging.

I'm not sure exactly when my exercise addiction hit, but I remember vividly the first month of my program, when I was still fighting inertia. I could hardly run around the block. I felt like my lungs would explode. My side ached. My legs ached, and I seriously questioned whether exercising was good for me.

Luckily, Joe was very patient and helped me set small, manageable goals. The first week I just struggled around the block. The second week I tried to run two blocks. I kept at it and slowly increased my blocks each week, but the only thing I really enjoyed the first couple of months was being able to stop jogging and come home to a nice hot shower. That's what felt good!

But somewhere between months four and six, I started really enjoying my morning runs. My side aches stopped and my legs got stronger. I found a park about six blocks away and loved jogging around a little lake. My energy increased, and I found that I wasn't so lethargic by the end of the workday.

It takes a while for most people to appreciate the pleasures of exercise—and at least four to six months to form a habit. For people who have never exercised or don't like to exercise, that means two things:

1. Sometimes you just have to make yourself do it.
2. You need to commit to doing it regularly and for several months.

If you continue exercising and make it a part of your life, not only will you feel better about yourself, but you'll also miss the days that you don't exercise. It's the best tonic I know. It renews, regenerates, and makes for increased vitality and energy!

TIPS ON GETTING STARTED AND MAKING EXERCISE A HABIT

1. *Remember the old Nike advertisements, "Just Do It."* To get started, you have to just do it. Pull out your calendar and block out 30 to 60 minutes three to four times a week. Pick your favorite and most convenient time of the day, and schedule your exercise time. At first some people feel that they just can't make time to exercise. They have meetings, conferences, projects, and relationships that need tending. I believe that if you take the time to exercise, you get more done because you have more energy and are more productive.

To help you get started, write *Just Do It* in your calendar to indicate your blocks of exercise time. Some people post their exercise schedules on their refrigerator and put a gold star over every segment they complete for positive reinforcement. The more they exercise, the more stars they get. Pretty soon the whole page is filled with stars. When you do this kind of thing, you feel better about yourself, and your self-confidence starts to improve.

2. *Change your ideas about exercise.* Some people think that exercise is a form of punishment or a penalty for bad behavior. Think instead that exercising means that you're taking more control of your life. You are exercising for your own physical, mental, and emotional health. It's your decision. Especially when job insecurities or life situations make us feel out of control, exercise is a perfect antidote. It puts us squarely in control of life, moving forward on our path.

3. *Make it fun.* Use your imagination and find ways to make exercise fun. I like to make up games while I'm running. Sometimes I pretend that I'm on safari and look for different birds and animals. I've spotted deer, coyotes, foxes, possums, and several inter-

esting birds. You can even pretend that you are the animal. Walk or run as they would. What would they be looking for? I'm reminded of how Merlin would change King Arthur into different animals to see how they lived and perceived the world. You certainly would have a different perspective. One time when I was running by San Francisco Bay, I spotted a shark swimming close to the shore. Sometimes I pretend that I'm wearing moccasins and running silently through the forest. Am I running from danger or running to dinner? I know some people who pick out a tree, rock, or other landmark, and pay tribute to it as they run or walk by. Use your imagination. Make up games. Have fun!

My friend Irene uses CDs and tapes to get her into the mood to exercise. The music keeps her exercise fresh and fun. Another friend listens to loud rock-and-roll music when she's doing aerobics or floor exercises. When she was training for a marathon, she would listen to tapes while running. One day she forgot her tapes and found herself singing the songs to her favorite tape over and over again.

4. *Say affirmations while you work out.* Use your exercise time to fill your mind with positive statements affirming your health, strength, and the goals you'd like to accomplish while you're working physically to remove tension and anxiety. Affirming while you're exercising can be very powerful. When Jim was going through a divorce and confused about his next career move, he wrote down twenty statements on 3 × 5 cards. He put them in his pocket and took them running, repeating each of them ten times. He wanted to work on finding a new job, a spacious new place to live, and a new car. He wanted to pay off his credit cards and have abundant energy to accomplish everything. These were his affirmations:

> *Because of my expertise, enthusiasm, compassion, and understanding, I am an incredibly successful real estate agent.*
> *I own a new Ford Mustang. I own my car free of debt.*

I have an unlimited supply of energy and can accomplish any-
   thing that I want to do.
My home is light, airy, spacious, and comfortable.
I am debt free.
I feel confident.

5. *Exercise outdoors and in scenic places.* Go out of your way to
find new paths and beautiful, interesting areas in your town. It's
hard to be bored when you're surrounded by beauty. My mother-
in-law lives in San Diego and used to drive down to the waterfront
to walk in the evening, watching the sun melt into the Pacific in
a trail of golden red light. My parents bicycle on a beautiful river
path in Montana that runs past the great falls that so intrigued
Lewis and Clark. Be on the lookout for interesting, beautiful trails
for hiking, walking, running, in-line skating, or biking. Use *when*
you exercise to your advantage as well. I like to run in the early
morning or just after sunset, when the light casts a golden hue.

6. *Don't overexert yourself.* Sometimes too much enthusiasm
can work against you. Trying to do everything too fast and too often can cause burnout and even injury. Pace yourself. Hopefully,
you'll have a lifetime to enjoy physical activity and meet all your
personal fitness goals.

7. *Find your own motivation.* Many experts claim that we're
motivated either by pain or by pleasure. I now know the pleasures
that come from exercising, but occasionally I need a little injec-
tion of pain to keep me going. On days when I'm too stressed or
too tired and would rather crawl back under the covers, I think
about what it would be like not to be able to walk or run. I remember reading *Johnny Got His Gun* in college. The Vietnam
War had just ended, and the book described a young World War
I soldier who had lost both of his arms and legs. He was still alive
but could never scratch his nose or walk again. I was so moved by
the story that when I finished reading it, I burst out of my dormi-

tory and started sprinting across the athletic field. I wanted to run as hard and as fast as I could. I wanted to use and really feel my legs. My greatest pain would be never to go on a hike again, never to go for a run.

Recently I've encountered a number of handicapped athletes: paraplegics in wheelchairs and blind runners speeding by in a race, blind skiers bravely venturing down a mountainside, and a mountain climber using only his arms and fine-tuned senses to climb the face of Half Dome in Yosemite National Park. I admire these athletes greatly. They have far more courage and determination than I have. They inspire me and help to keep me running on days when I'd rather stay at home. I think that if they can do it, so can I.

8. *Find a role model*, someone who's already in shape, physically fit, and has an abundance of energy. Benefit from the guidance of seasoned athletes. Learn from their experiences. Find out how often they exercise, what they do for exercise, how long they exercise, even what types of food they eat. We can all be inspired by people who have an abundance of energy and look terrific.

Working out with other people can also be a great motivator and tremendous fun. I now go on long walks with my friend Carolyn. After walking and talking for an hour, I feel that I've had the best therapy session in the world. Check out fitness magazines for people who look great and see how they do it. Magazines are a wonderful place to find role models. The pictures alone can be very motivational. If you can't find a personal role model, then subscribe to a fitness or sporting magazine or join an outdoor group or exercise class that interests you. You're bound to meet some very interesting people and learn some great tips from them.

9. *Check with your doctor before beginning any exercise program*, especially if you've led a sedentary life, are overweight, have high blood pressure, and/or have medical problems or a family history of medical problems.

AEROBIC EXERCISE FOR MENTAL CLARITY

Aerobic exercise three to four times a week reduces the harmful effects of stress, helps you think more clearly, and gives you more energy. It helps your whole body run more efficiently and, along with an adequate amount of sleep and a healthy low-fat diet, is essential to functioning at your personal best.

Aerobic means "in the presence of oxygen," and any type of aerobic exercise promotes better circulation of blood and oxygen to all parts of the body, including the brain, so that you think more clearly.

The goal of an aerobics fitness program is to do a minimum of 30 minutes of continuous exercise at 70 to 80 percent of your maximum heart rate at least three or four days a week. All exercise should include warm-up and cool-down periods with some stretching.

Floor exercises, light calisthenics, and weight training help to strengthen and tone muscles but are not considered aerobic. Aerobic exercise uses large muscles rhythmically and continuously and elevates the heart rate and breathing for a sustained period.

HOW TO DETERMINE YOUR MAXIMUM HEART RATE AND SUGGESTED WORKOUT INTENSITY

Count the beat of your pulse for 10 seconds immediately after you've stopped exercising, using the tips of your fingers and a stopwatch, clock, or wristwatch with a second hand. The best places to find your pulse are on the inside of your wrist or on your neck behind your Adam's apple. Multiply that number by six to get your heart rate per minute.

Most physical fitness experts recommend that you work at a heart rate of 70 to 80 percent of your maximum heart rate.

If you're just beginning an exercise program, you should try to work at 50 to 60 percent of your maximum heart rate. To find your maximum heart rate, subtract your age from 220. For example, if you are 40 years old, your maximum heart rate is 180.

$$220 - 40 = 180$$

Since you should be working at between 70 and 80 percent of your maximum heart rate, your rate at the end of an exercise session should be between 126 and 144. This is often referred to as your exercise target zone.

$$180 \times .7 = 126, \text{ or a 10-second count of 21}$$
$$180 \times .8 = 144, \text{ or a 10-second count of 24}$$

ENVIRONMENTAL AEROBIC WORKOUTS

Some great activities for achieving aerobic fitness are running, jogging, swimming, cycling, cross-country skiing, aerobic dancing, rowing, in-line skating, hiking, and walking at a brisk pace. Obviously, not all of these activities can be done outdoors and in quiet, peaceful places. Since fresh air helps to cleanse and oxygenate the cells and tissues and natural light helps to revitalize our bodies, here are a few aerobic activities that can be done outside and don't require special equipment. Exercising outdoors enables you to enjoy all the benefits of aerobic exercise plus the added benefits of the beauty, grandeur, and quiet majesty of nature.

Walking

Walking is a great exercise and can be lots of fun. You can explore new worlds and at the same time spend time thinking about the new life that you want to create. You can walk almost anywhere: in parks, interesting neighborhoods, and even shopping malls when it's too cold to walk outside. Since walking is typically not a strenuous workout, most health experts agree that you should try to walk briskly and at a fast pace to achieve the aerobic benefits.

Getting started: If you've never exercised before or haven't exercised in a while, start by walking at a comfortable pace and increase your distance and pace gradually. Begin walking three or four days a week for 30 minutes and gradually increase the time. You can pick up your pace by taking longer strides and walking faster. I find that I walk faster when I move my arms faster. Walking briskly up hills can also increase your heart rate. Your goal should be to increase your walking time to 60 minutes four or five days a week.

Take a wristwatch or stopwatch with you and stop to take your pulse every 10 minutes in the beginning. When you're first getting started, you might want to alternate between walking briskly and walking slower until you can sustain a brisk walking pace. Be sure to stretch before and after your workout session.

Hiking

Hiking is basically walking, but it is usually done on nature trails with more rugged terrain and sometimes includes steep hills, so it's important to have shoes that provide traction and good support for your ankles. I've gone hiking in low-tread sneakers and found myself slipping and sliding down hills. It wasn't a lot of fun. As with walking, you need to hike at a brisk pace to achieve aerobic benefits. If you're lucky enough to have hilly terrain in your area, you can increase your heart rate faster. Hiking with weights or a heavy backpack can also help increase your heart rate in a shorter period of time. Always be on the lookout for loose gravel so that you don't twist or sprain your ankle. I find hiking to be one of the most scenic and enjoyable forms of exercise.

Getting started: Start hiking at a comfortable pace. Many trailheads start on level ground, and this is a good area to warm up. Once you have warmed up, hike at a brisk pace and take your pulse regularly to make sure that you reach your target heart rate. Practice breathing deeply, even going uphill! Hikers should begin hiking a minimum of 30 minutes three or four times a week, and increase their hiking time to 60 minutes four or five times a week. Remember to take plenty of water with you and to do warm-up and cooldown exercises before and after your hike. Enjoy the scenery!

Walk/Jog

Many experts advise that you shouldn't start jogging until you can walk briskly for three miles with ease. A walk combined with jogging is an excellent way to ease into jogging or simply to increase your pulse rate while continuing to enjoy the pleasures of walking. During a walk/jog, start with walking. When you're warmed up, jog for a short distance and then resume walking. Jogging can be hard on your joints, so make sure that you don't jog too fast and always wear good running shoes.

Getting started: To begin, start walking slowly to warm up and gradually increase your pace. Once you feel comfortable, begin to jog slowly. Jog the distance of about one city block and then resume walking. Try to insert three to four jogs into a 30-minute walk. When you're first starting to jog, take your pulse every 10 minutes and again at the end of your workout. Your goal should be to elevate your heart rate to your target zone and at the same time enjoy your workout. Generally, you can achieve cardiovascular benefits with a combination of walking and jogging for 30 minutes three or four times a week. Check your pulse!

Jogging

Jogging is recognized as one of the best ways to develop and maintain cardiovascular fitness. The goal is to jog 30 minutes three or four days a week. I love to jog and always feel energized afterward, but I know a number of people who don't jog either because they have injured themselves jogging or because they fear injuries. Since jogging can be very addictive, I've known a few people who have been injured and just kept on doing it. One of my good friends injured his foot jogging and did not allow it time to heal. The result was that he permanently damaged his foot and can never jog again. Most injuries happen when you jog too fast, too far, or too soon—or when you don't wear proper running shoes.

Getting started: It's easy to get started jogging by practicing a walk/jog routine first and gradually increasing your jogging distance until you are jogging more than you are walking. Make sure that your shoulders, hips, knees, and feet are all aligned when you jog. You should have a natural gait and not be too tense. Sometimes I check out my posture as I run by store windows that act almost as mirrors. Some people work too hard when they jog, with movements that aren't fluid. It truly can be an art. If you're having problems, check with a fitness expert. They can videotape your run and pinpoint problems immediately. If you become overly tense while you're jogging, shake it out.

Try to jog a minimum of 30 minutes three times a week. Alternate jog days with rest days in the beginning, since your body needs time to rest and recover, and remember to do warm-up and cool-down exercises before and after a jog.

CLOTHING AND SHOES

Make sure that you wear comfortable shoes and clothing. You warm up quickly when exercising, and it's best to layer clothing so that you can control your body temperature. Many new fabrics let sweat evaporate, keep the rain out, and are windproof. Check the labels or ask a salesclerk. In cold weather, try wearing a jacket with big pockets so that you can stuff clothing in them after you warm up. If you're planning to bicycle, you might want to consider purchasing some lightweight clothing. Some of the colors and styles are fun and outrageous!

Shoes should provide you with good cushioning and support. Many companies now make shoes that have been especially designed for walking, running, cycling, or hiking. You can check out various types and brand names in *Consumer Reports* or consult with an expert before making a purchase. Try on your new shoes with the same thickness of sock that you'll be wearing during your workout. Walk around in the store for a few minutes to make sure the shoes feel comfortable. A good and comfortable running, cycling, walking, or hiking shoe should give you good support and help you avoid injuries.

TEN WAYS TO HAVE FUN WHILE YOU EXERCISE

1. Work out with a friend. It's always fun to share a beautiful walk, hike, bike, or run with a friend. Find someone who is upbeat and a good listener, and you'll come back refreshed and invigorated. Don't forget to be a good listener yourself.

2. Work out in beautiful areas. Scout them out in advance. During your walk, take "inspirational" breaks. Stop and smell the flowers, admire a view, or feel the energy from a tree.

3. Make your workouts an adventure. Discover new areas. I like to start by making a list of ten areas that I've never explored and are within 20 miles of where I live. I try to exercise in one of these areas at least once a month. Go on a safari. Look for animal tracks and new flora and fauna. Keep a log of all your new discoveries.

4. Write down 10 to 15 affirmations on 3 × 5 note cards and take them with you. Be sure to include your abundance and health affirmations. While you exercise, say them each ten times. Choose affirmations that pump you up and raise your self-esteem and confidence.

5. *Wear clothing that makes you feel good about yourself.* Sometimes the clothes do make the man or woman. Sally found that the grungier the clothes she wore while exercising, the grungier she felt. Sometimes she didn't even want to leave the house. Consider buying a new outfit that makes you feel terrific!

6. *Reward yourself for sticking to your exercise program.* Chart your schedule and progress on a calendar and display it prominently. Every week that you meet your goals, reward yourself. Buy something that makes you feel special or good. See Chapter 3 for some ideas. On weekends I like to run early in the morning and then make a wonderful breakfast or go out to breakfast. It's my little reward and a great way to start the day.

7. *Take a Silence and Solitude hike, walk, or run at least once a week.* Go alone and try to remove yourself from as many people and man-made noises as possible. If you need to decide something, pose it as a question. This is a great time to hear your wise inner voice.

8. *Buy a cassette or CD player and listen to great music while working out.* Make sure that the music has a good beat and helps you feel energetic. This is not the time for sad and somber music. Consider putting together your own workout tape.

9. *Make a mental list of all the things for which you are grateful.* While you're exercising, review your list. You can think about things that happened last week, last month, or last year. You can even review your entire life.

10. *Daydream about the new life that you're going to create.* Visualize what you want to be doing and where you want to live and work.

Greg is a member of a health club in downtown San Francisco. He tries to lift weights two times a week after work. During his Clarity Quest, he decided to add 20 minutes of running to his weight-training schedule.

Greg's health club is in the heart of the city and surrounded by high-rises, but within a few minutes Greg could get to a path that ran alongside the bay. While he was running, he would look out at the bay and watch sailboats go by, ships come in, and the beautiful light of sunset. He found the run to be both calming and exhilarating. He started hiking early Saturday mornings on Mount Tamalpais and discovered it was a great way to completely escape his daily stresses. While he was running and hiking, he found that he was able to easily solve problems that had perplexed him at work. By the end of Week #4, Greg felt strong and healthy and ready to tackle some big changes in his life.

CLARITY INSIGHT #5

Daydreams reveal what's possible.

Our daydreams can help us get in touch with our hopes, desires, and potential. They don't necessarily reveal the future, but they offer us a glimpse of what could happen.

Remembering your daydreams can be a lot of fun. Put on a pot of tea. Have a glass of wine. Kick off your shoes and think like a child. Allow your imagination to be expansive. What did you dream about when you were a child? What kind of life did you want? What did you imagine yourself doing? Think about your dreams when you were a teenager, a young adult, and an adult. What are your current dreams? Don't analyze them, just write them down. How different are your dreams from your current life? Spend some time thinking about your daydreams and whether they can offer you any guidance and future direction. Take a break. Go for a walk. Get involved in a project or hobby. When insights occur, write them down and highlight them in your journal.

Consider starting a "dream file." Fill it with things that you admire and fantasize about. Your file might include how you want to look, what you want to wear, what you want to be doing, and where you want to live and work.

WEEK 4 ACTIVITIES AND EXERCISES

Remember to take a cleansing shower each morning.

Sunday

- Take a Silence and Solitude break. Find a quiet, peaceful location and spend at least 20 minutes there alone. Be still and observe the sights around you.
- Complete Clarity Insight #5.
- Review your calendar and map out activities for the week.
- Buy healthy foods for the week.
- Choose exercises for the week and map out your exercise route.

Monday

- Meditate 20 to 30 minutes.
- Exercise.

Tuesday

- Find a quiet place outdoors and practice a breathing exercise.
- Create two or three verbal affirmations. Think vitality, vigor, and increased energy. Add to existing affirmations and repeat 10 times daily.

Wednesday

- Meditate 20 to 30 minutes.
- Exercise.

Thursday

- Take a Beauty break.

Friday

- Meditate 20 to 30 minutes.
- Exercise.

Saturday

- Take an early-morning walk with your Clarity Quest buddy.
- Complete your Progress Report and reward yourself for completing Base Camp Training. You should be feeling more calm, rested, and relaxed, with a heightened sense of physical well-being and increased energy.
- Take a time-out. Celebrate the positive changes that are happening in your life. Brew a cup of tea, open a bottle of champagne, and celebrate how much you've accomplished these first few weeks. Reflect on what you've accomplished and how much better you're feeling.

PROGRESS REPORT

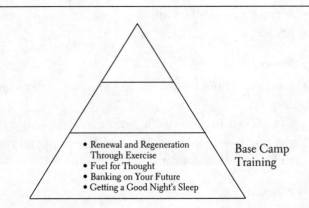

Base Camp Training

- Renewal and Regeneration Through Exercise
- Fuel for Thought
- Banking on Your Future
- Getting a Good Night's Sleep

- What did you accomplish this week?
- How are you feeling? Healthier? More energetic? Better about yourself? More in control? More confident?
- Have you found a place for your getaway? If not, continue researching.

Record your feelings and insights in your journal.

Part Two

LIGHTENING THE LOAD

Chapter 6

Week 5: Simplifying and Streamlining Your Life

▦ *We were told to swim out about 50 yards to a buoy before we began our descent. What a shock! The water was ice cold, and I tried to swim as fast as I could, flailing my arms and legs to try to keep warm. Big mistake. By the time I reached the buoy, I'd used up most of my energy and had to wait for all the experienced divers to catch up. They took their time—slowly and gracefully making their way out to the buoy.*

During our descent I hugged myself and shivered under the water to let the dive master know that I was cold—freezing, actually. My lips were numb, and I was worried about keeping the regulator in my mouth. He tested me first so I could head back. I was very nervous, which I know consumed even more of my precious energy. I had a hard time getting back to the shore, even though I was swimming underwater this time and it should have been easier. Lots of people passed me by as I struggled with the current. By the time I reached the shore, it felt as though several hours had passed. I crawled out of the water and fell facedown into the sand. I couldn't get up and I didn't care.

We had to complete three more ocean dives that weekend to get certified. I didn't feel that I had the energy to stand up, let alone dive again. Thank God the dive master came over to talk to me. If he hadn't shared a few simple tips, I would not have gone back in the water, wouldn't have gotten certified, and would have missed out on some of the most beautiful adventures of my life.

— JOURNAL ENTRY

The value of energy conservation hit home during that first ocean dive in Monterey. I lost a lot of body heat in that cold water, but most of my energy had been depleted by overexerting myself. I had exhausted myself by swimming too fast and working too hard. The second day of diving was easy and effortless, simply because the dive master gave me a few tips and I followed them!

On the drive home I thought about his advice and realized that it applied to other areas of life as well. His four valuable diving tips can help conserve time and energy at work, at home, at play, and in every other aspect of living:

- *Simplify* by not overextending.
- *Streamline your movements.*
- *Chart your direction* and follow it.
- *Stop, think, and act* whenever you're out of control, panicked, or heading in the wrong direction.

How many times have you heard people say, "I just don't have enough time in one day to get everything done?" or "I feel so rushed and scattered, I can't seem to accomplish anything?" As we juggle the demands of work, family, and social commitments, there are times when most of us wish we had a few extra hours in the day. Ironically, it's not *time* that we need more of—it's *focus*.

When we have a clear focus and direction for each day, we don't scatter our energy and we have more than enough time to accomplish everything that we want. It's easy for our lives to become cluttered and seem out of control. We keep adding and adding and adding and never subtracting. It's easy to feel scattered, overwhelmed, and unable to take action.

The goal this week is to free up more time and energy by simplifying and streamlining your life and by becoming more focused, organized, and efficient.

WEEK 5 OBJECTIVE

To Free Up More Time and Energy by Becoming More
Focused, Organized, and Efficient

This week you'll learn:

- ✔ How to stop feeling overwhelmed, rushed, and scattered
- ✔ Techniques for cleaning out the clutter and clearing away
  the old to make way for new and better things in your life

SIMPLIFY

There are many ways we can simplify our lives and avoid overextending ourselves. Here are a few of the most basic.

Pull in Scattered Energy

Sometimes we don't realize just how scattered we are until we stop and look at a list of our daily activities. Are there any activities in your schedule that could be more organized, simple, or efficient? I kept a log of daily activities to see if there were more efficient ways to do things and discovered that changing just a few things saved hours every day—giving me more time for play, creative expression, and the people I love.

Try keeping a log of your daily activities and see if they can be streamlined. Here are some examples:

ACTIVITY	TIME	WHAT TO DO FOR MORE EFFICIENCY	THINGS TO DO WITH THE EXTRA TIME
Getting ready for work	1 hour	Make coffee night before. Have clothes ironed and ready. *Time Saved: 15 minutes*	Exercise Read newspaper. Sleep in!
Commuting	1½ hours	Leave 30 minutes earlier to avoid bottleneck traffic. *Time Saved: 20 minutes*	Take longer lunch. Exercise at lunch. Have more quiet time at work before phones start ringing.
Phone calls	3 hours	Set agenda and time limit for scheduled conference calls. Limit nonessential calls by saying you only have a few minutes to talk. Set time limit, especially for non-work-related calls or with people you know will be long-winded. *Time Saved: 1 hour*	Visit with friends in more relaxed setting after work. Go shopping. Take a long walk.
Meetings	2 hours	Limit time for each agenda item. Tell facilitator in advance that you need to leave on time. Make late-comers read minutes or stay later to hear what they missed. *Time Saved: 1 hour*	Finish work at office rather than bringing it home.

Running errands	1 hour	Stop at store on way home. Make shopping list and coordinate errand running to one part of town, one shopping complex. *Time Saved: 30 minutes*	Walk dogs. Garden. Read a book. Call a friend.
Cooking & cleaning up	1 hour	If there are two or more people in your household, divide tasks. If one person cooks, the other cleans up. *Time Saved: 30 minutes*	Play piano. Listen to tapes. Watch television.

The total time saved in one day is more than 3½ hours. That averages out to about 17 hours a week, or 60-some hours a month. That's a lot of precious time.

There is usually a simpler, more organized, more efficient way to do any task. By paying attention to your activities and where you waste time or energy, you can create more time in each day to do the things you really love doing. A few simple changes can save you several hours each week.

Some of the biggest energy wasters during the day are driving time, phone time, meeting time, unexpected interruptions, reading mail, memos, e-mail, and taking on too many commitments. Simplifying just a few of these activities can save you many hours.

Driving Time

When I was young, I would go shopping with my grandmother. She lived on a farm about thirty miles from town and would stop by our house to visit with my parents and pick me up. Grandma was a big bargain hunter and would drive around to a half-dozen stores just to check out prices before she bought anything. One time we shopped for about two hours for an item, only to return to the first store and purchase it. Grandma only saved a dollar that day, but she was happy. My father would shake his head and try to tell her that her time, plus the cost of gasoline, was worth a lot more than the money she saved by driving all over. He was right, even in those days, and the principle applies even more today. Our time is so precious that it pays to "let your fingers do the walking" in the Yellow Pages before you leave home—especially if you know exactly what you want.

Even when you are just shopping to check out the new styles and see what's in season, you can save time by parking once and shopping in a downtown area or shopping mall to investigate what's hot and what's not. Many people window-shop before they buy so that they have a clear idea of what they're looking for. Before you leave the house, spend some time making lists of what you need and where you're going so that you can run errands more efficiently. You'll save time by mapping out a route and, whenever possible, running all the errands in one part of town at the same time.

If you drive to work, explore more efficient ways to get there. Public transportation can be wonderful because you can sit back, relax, work, read, or even doze on your way to work. If you have to drive, you can utilize that time as well. Many people listen to books on tape or use their car phone to check voice mail. Others use their driving time to unwind mentally. They put on a relaxing audiotape or just use the time to assimilate what happened during the day. If you're wrestling with a problem, let it sit on the back burner during this time. Try posing the issue as a simple question. Relax and listen to the music. You'll often have a solution by the time you get home.

Phone Calls, Mail, and Meetings

I've heard people say that about half of all the time spent at work is wasted on phone calls, mail, meetings, and interruptions. Many of these activities are a necessary part of business, but they often take longer than necessary, and it's easy to get sidetracked.

Here's an exercise that you may find revealing. Whenever you're in a meeting or get a phone call, keep track of how much time is spent on business. People-oriented people love catching up on what's happening in other people's lives, but if you limit yourself to a few pleasantries and set some time boundaries, you can enjoy the same personal connection and still use your time more effectively. As a result, you'll have more time to get out a report or have a pleasant lunch with one of your colleagues.

If you're extremely busy, tell callers that you don't have time to talk right now and ask them if there's a good time for you to call them back. If it's urgent, they'll let you know. Another technique is to set time limits. Let people know that you can spare only five minutes right now and that you can either talk now or get back to them later. Setting these parameters gives you more control over your time.

Many people consider telemarketing calls an invasion of their time and energy. My friend Rita says that when someone calls her and can't pronounce her name, she simply asks if it is a telemarketing call. If the answer is yes, Rita politely says that she doesn't like telemarketing calls at home or at the office and asks that her name be removed from the caller's list. It works! It takes very little time, and it's amazing how easy it is to take control.

Meetings are a necessary part of doing business, but most meetings run longer than anyone imagines and are far less focused than anyone would like to think. Sometimes they seem to take on a life of their own.

If you're running the meeting, you definitely have more control. Anna works for a software development company. She sends out an agenda for each meeting to everyone participating, with time allocations for each subject to be discussed. She also writes the agenda and time allotments on a flip chart in the room. At the start of the meeting, she reviews the agenda and makes sure everyone agrees to the priorities and time allocations. Priority items are always discussed first. When the time for discussing a certain subject is over, additional discussion is either tabled until a later date or sent to a subcommittee.

If you're attending a meeting, you can tell the facilitator in advance that you have to leave at the specified time—and that if the meeting runs longer, you would like a copy of the minutes.

Inevitably, someone shows up late for a meeting and has to be briefed on what's happened. Try not to reward these people for being late. I've witnessed some excellent facilitators simply acknowledge their entrance and tell them that they'll fill them in after the meeting is over. If people know you're going to start on time, they are more likely to show up on time so that they don't miss anything important. You might even consider having coffee and snacks prior to the meeting so that those who want time to socialize and catch up can do so. It's a nice reward for coming early.

Reading and writing mail and memos can also be great time and energy wasters. The information age keeps us busy reading and responding to hundreds of items each day. Not only do we have regular mail, but now we must read and respond to faxes and e-mail. Try sorting through mail and e-mail messages to determine what's important, and then throw out or delete what's not important. Save or print only what needs attention.

Janice sorts through all this material and files it in one of three brightly colored folders on her desk. Anything that needs immediate action goes into her yellow folder. Anything that requires action within the week goes into her green file. Future reading goes in her blue file. She tries to tackle all the yellow material before she leaves the office each day, and reviews what's in her green file each morning and evening to determine what needs to be moved to the yellow file. Her blue file is available whenever she feels like reading something of interest or has the time to file the material away.

Many people have told me that they used to spend a great deal of time trying to write the perfect memo. They would agonize over words rather than thinking about the key points they wanted to make. The solution was learning to take a few minutes to think about what they wanted to say, then mapping out the key points and quickly drafting the memo. Books like Richard Andersen's *Writing That Works* can help streamline your writing.

Interruptions

A good friend recently complained that she could never get any serious work done in the office because of constant interruptions and drop-ins. If people just drop into your office, there's nothing wrong with telling them that you'd love to talk but that you can spare only a few minutes. Specify an amount of time you can chat with them, refer to your watch, and when the time's up, tell them you need to get back to work. I've noticed lately that many people put up signs on their computer screens or on their doors to let others know that they're on a conference call and can't be interrupted or that they need some serious concentration time to tackle a problem.

When my friend Sam is under the gun to get something done, he takes his work with him to a library or conference room and doesn't tell anyone where he's going. He just lets them know when he'll be back. When I was writing this book, I designated several mornings a week to do nothing else but work on the book. I let the answering machine pick up calls and took myself away from all other interruptions. Sometimes I even headed to the park for hours of thinking and writing.

Taking on Too Many Commitments

This is a difficult area for many people. They become interested in a variety of projects and get recruited to head up task forces, volunteer groups, and neighborhood fund-raising efforts. They love to try new things and meet new people and have a hard time saying no. They frequently overbook and as a result are either stretched too thin or constantly running late.

A few years ago there was an antidrug campaign that advertised, "Just say no." At the time I had a full-time job, belonged to a health club, did volunteer work for the symphony, and visited an elderly person in a nursing home one day a week. I had just started going to night school to get my MBA, and my stepchildren were living with us on the weekends. It was too much. I was overcommitted and overwhelmed. Something had to give. I was quickly becoming a basket case because I just didn't say no. Somehow it seemed like saying no to life.

Driving home late one night, the "Just say no" message really hit home. Saying no to drugs enables you to be in control. Saying no to some of my activities would help me gain more control of my life. I knew that I would disappoint a few people, but if I didn't scale back, I'd ultimately disappoint myself, my close friends, and my family—the people who mattered to me. They were more of a priority than outside projects or even school.

In addition to practicing saying no, it helps simply to tell the truth. If you tell the truth to yourself, you'll know what to cut out and where to scale back. If you tell the truth to others, you can honestly say why you can't participate in something or why you can spend only a few minutes with them. Sometimes people want more of us than we're able to give, and a few may respond negatively to your honesty. Friends may be disappointed when you scale back on lunches or cut out activities that you did together regularly—but unless you are honest with them and firm about how much time you have to give, you may be disappointed in yourself and resentful of those friendships.

Life is a balancing act, but if you strive to be true to yourself and true to others, you can learn to carry just the right load.

Less Is More

Carol, an attractive and vibrant brunette, has one of the most beautifully decorated homes that I've ever seen. Everything in it is bright and lively and engaging. The problem is that there's so much "stuff" that it's hard to focus on any one item. The last time I visited with her, I even found it hard to focus on our conversation. My eyes kept wandering to the colorful pictures on the walls, the interesting books, and the decorative art pieces and gadgets on the coffee table, bookshelves, and fireplace mantel. Almost every inch was covered with something. I was intrigued by her house but not at peace there. My mind was constantly distracted.

Carol decided to remove some of the clutter and found that having fewer things in her house helped free up some of her energy. She didn't have to spend so much time caring for her things.

Many of our "things" are a joy to have, but the more things we have, the more of our energy is tied up in their cost, care, and maintenance. During the Yuppie boom of the early 1980s, I lived in Marin County, north of San Francisco. Everyone seemed to want more. More home, more car, more toys, more things. It took almost an entire decade for many people to realize that sometimes having more meant less. Less freedom, less time, and sometimes less fun.

To keep up with the payments, people had to work harder and longer each day. No wonder so many people gave up after a while and moved to smaller communities, made less money, had fewer things, and yet ultimately had much more — more time, more freedom, more control over their lives, and more fun.

Many of our things do bring joy to us. Be sensitive to what those things are and choose them carefully. Most things in life need some level of care and maintenance and can require a lot of your precious time and energy.

Clean Up the Clutter and Streamline

One of the most effective ways to streamline your life is to eliminate clutter. In college my freshman roommate and I lived quite happily in a room that looked as though a cyclone had hit it. Papers, notebooks, flyers, and clothes lay strewn across the desktops and floor. It took us forever just to get ready in the morning. We couldn't find anything. We'd frantically rummage through the clothes pile on the floor for five minutes just to locate a favorite pair of jeans. It would take an additional five minutes to locate the shampoo, the coffee cup, and a paper that was due at an 11:00 class. Our disorganization cost us valuable time, and we were both nearly hysterical by midterms.

The time we spent trying to find things took a lot of study time, so we stayed up later and later each night. My roommate's mother visited us the week before midterms and insisted that we clean up our room. Thank God. She explained that we'd never be able to concentrate on our exams unless we had some order in our room. We were desperate, so under her guidance we spent all day Saturday picking up, sorting, filing, and organizing. It worked! We were able to focus and concentrate only on studying. To this day I'm amazed at how easy it is to focus and concentrate on the task at hand when other things aren't screaming at you for your attention. It was a valuable lesson. When I'm out of sorts and can't seem to get anything done, my first priority is to get organized and clean up my mess.

REASONS TO ORGANIZE AND CLEAN YOUR HOME AND WORK ENVIRONMENT

1. *An organized external environment lets you focus more easily on the task at hand.* When clutter and half-done projects lie all over your desk, it's easy to get distracted and never recover from that confused and overwhelmed state of mind. Your concentration becomes scattered. Cleaning up and organizing help you to become more streamlined and productive. Some part of your mind pays attention to everything in your environment. When you simplify that environment, your mind can concentrate on the important things. You become much more efficient and effective. Especially when your mind is in a chaotic state, your environment should be neat and clean.

2. *Taking action can be very therapeutic* when you feel muddled or discombobulated. A good friend of mine vacuums her

house whenever she feels confused or fearful. She claims that vacuuming helps her get up and out of her paralyzed state of mind. *Doing* something, rather than *dwelling* on something, helps dissolve fears, worries, and confusion. Cleaning, organizing, and simplifying are all actions that can help keep you calm.

3. *When you clear out the old, you make way for the new.* It's hard to attract anything new into your life when your current space is cluttered or filled. When you create an empty space, you make room for new people, ideas, or things to come into your life.

A former roommate of mine wanted to find the man of her dreams, but frankly, she didn't have the time or space for someone new to enter her life. She was booked solid with work and existing obligations with family and friends. Another friend wanted his girlfriend to move in with him. He talked about it a lot, but he never actually cleaned out space in his closets for her to move her things in. She even said that if he cleared some space for her, she would move in. He never got around to it, and they soon parted.

You've probably heard the expression "Nature abhors a vacuum." If you take time to clear some space in your life, it will fill up again. By getting rid of what you no longer want, you create a space for things you do want. This holds true for possessions, people, and ideas.

An added benefit of getting rid of things is that you can make money by selling them in a consignment store or at a garage sale. Everyone I know who's had a garage sale is amazed at how much money they make. What they considered junk, someone else considered a treasure! The items that you don't sell you can give away to charity.

4. *Cleaning, straightening, and organizing give you a feeling of accomplishment.* It feels good to start something and finish it. Karl works in product marketing, and sometimes it takes his group two years to introduce a product. In his line of work, he

rarely has the satisfaction of seeing something started and finished in a timely manner. It's not hard to understand why one of his real joys in life is to complete projects around the house and yard. He's often able to begin a task and see the results in one weekend. I feel the same way about cleaning the house. Seeing immediate results and having everything clean and orderly makes me feel great.

Tips for Annual Organizing and Spring Cleaning

Make a master list of rooms in your house and record what needs to be cleaned or gotten rid of in each one. Having a master checklist is great because it keeps you on track and focused—and also enables you to check off items when you've completed them! That's great motivation for many people.

Try tackling only one room a day and setting a specific amount of time to clean. Some people like to move very methodically, dealing with one file drawer or corner at a time. If you move from area to area or room to room, you may waste a great deal of energy and feel scattered. My friend Pat loves to play her favorite tapes while reading articles, letters, and memos that she's set aside to toss. She brews a great cup of tea and really enjoys her morning or afternoon. Many people combine cleaning out the clutter with spring cleaning. Generally, spring cleaning should be done at least once a year, but if you're a real pack rat and have a lot of items to wade through, you might want to toss out items in the fall and do your heavy cleaning in the spring.

As a rule, if you haven't used an item in the last three years, toss it out. The only exceptions are tax records and items that have a sentimental meaning for you.

Office Organizing

You may need to go through your files at least twice a year to discard unimportant information. Here are three tips for reviewing and cleaning out files:

1. Check with the IRS or your accountant to find out how long you need to keep certain files. If you keep all past tax records in cardboard file boxes and date the boxes, you can throw out the entire box when that period runs out.
2. Toss out all dated information, papers, brochures, and catalogs that are more than three years old. Put articles or clippings that you've been meaning to read in a basket for later.
3. Put all garage sale items in a separate box. Schedule the garage sale within a month. If you wait too long, you may never get around to having one.

Organizing and Cleaning Out Closets and Drawers

When Sally cleans out her closets and drawers, she puts on lively music and has a fashion show—for herself. She puts on all her outfits that are at least three years old and decides which clothes she wants to keep. Some people even take Polaroid shots of their private fashion show. Be critical. Do you really look good in that old wool suit? Is it hopelessly outdated? Toss old clothes and shoes into a big bag that's ready for the garage sale, the consignment store, or charity.

Remember, you have only so much closet space. When that space is full, it's probably time to clean it out so that you can make way for new items. Remove the old to make way for the new. Once you've decided which items you're going to keep, organize them in your closet according to purpose. Designate one area for dresses, another for slacks, one for suits, and so on. It saves a lot of time in the morning because you can go directly to the appropriate part of the closet.

Consider going through your wardrobe twice a year to assess your fall/winter and spring/summer clothing. This is a good time to check which clothing needs mending, buttons sewn on, hems shortened, or dry cleaning.

Cleaning out the clutter—and just plain old cleaning—gives you a feeling of satisfaction and control in your life. There's a great sense of accomplishment in simply starting and finishing a project. Once the clutter is removed, you'll be ready to eliminate other energy wasters and focus on creating your blueprint for the future!

CLEAR FOCUS AND DIRECTION FOR EACH DAY

Our day-to-day distractions can be like strong currents that pull us in different directions and keep us from reaching our destination. To head in the direction that you choose to go, rather than in the direction the currents take you, requires a bit of advance planning, organization, and focus.

The ultimate tool for staying focused and on the right path is to have clearly defined goals. They become like a compass or lighthouse beacon that helps you to navigate, stay on course, and always move in the right direction.

By the end of this program, you'll have some clearly defined goals to help you prioritize day-to-day activities and weed out things that aren't important. In the meantime, the exercises in this chapter will help you free up more time and energy by becoming more efficient and more focused.

Tips to Help You Organize Your Day

A good friend of mine epitomizes the truly organized person. I've had the good fortune to work with him and observe his work habits. He always appears calm and focused, does quality work, gets it done on time, and leaves early every night. His colleagues, on the other hand, are often rushing around looking harried, harassed, and scattered. They routinely work late and often have to take work home with them. I've found many of his tips invaluable and share them here with you.

At the End of the Day

1. Spend 15 minutes at the end of each day visualizing and preparing for tomorrow. Before going home, my friend reviews and revises his To Do list. In the course of the day, he has added a number of miscellaneous items to his list and spends a few minutes reviewing and prioritizing everything he's jotted down. He determines how much time each activity will take. He also takes a look at his calendar to see his schedule for the next day. Then he closes his eyes and begins to picture in his mind the desired results for the next day. He thinks about what absolutely must get done and how to best structure his day to make sure he has enough time to accomplish these essential tasks. He pictures himself completing all these activities in a calm and efficient manner.

To prioritize his tasks, my friend evaluates whether they are helping him meet his goals and objectives. If you're consistently doing activities that don't have anything to do with your goals, then either you're doing the wrong activities or you should rethink your goals. I know many people who take on task after task in the spirit of helpfulness or special interest and find at the end of the year that they have failed to meet their objectives. Sometimes the ramifications can be quite severe, like disappointing raises or poor performance reviews.

2. Think about what you can do to free up your energy. Some tasks are unpleasant, and we try to avoid doing them as long as possible—things like calling back an unhappy customer, confronting a co-worker, making a cold call, or completing an expense report. These are tasks that you eventually have to do. The longer you postpone them, the longer they linger in the back of your mind and waste your energy. If you tackle these items right away, you'll not only feel great but will free up a lot of energy.

Also think about what tasks can be deleted or delegated. Would anyone really notice if you didn't do this item? Would anyone notice if you didn't attend a meeting? Could you delegate a few of your activities?

3. *Try not to take work home.* Having a balanced life means being able to detach from work and focus on other important areas: family, recreation, relaxation, spiritual life, and social activities. You are more productive at work if you approach what you're doing in a calm and relaxed manner. If work is your only outlet for expression and creativity, you can start to take it too seriously. You can become too intense, lose perspective, and not see the forest for the trees. All work and no play can be very unhealthy.

At the Beginning of Each Day

1. *Spend 15 minutes visualizing a smooth, productive, crisis-free day.* Visualize important projects, meetings, and phone calls happening exactly the way you'd like them to unfold. Spend time thinking about how you want your day to be so that your thoughts focus on accomplishing those things and you don't get derailed by outside events.

During the Day

1. *Focus on the task at hand.* Give whatever you are doing your full attention. Remove all distractions. Some people clean off their desk and organize their files every day before going home. Practicing meditation helps sharpen your ability to concentrate.

2. *Take breaks during the day.* Breaks help restore your energy. Just taking a quick break and going outside for a few minutes can help you to reassess what's important and what's not. When you're mired in a complex project, try going for a walk or a run. Come back refreshed and ready to focus fully on the activity at hand.

Try this organizational approach for a few days. Be aware of which activities move you closer to your goals and which do not. Remember, the currents will pull you off your path if you let them.

Explore how to eliminate tasks that don't keep you headed in the direction you want to go.

STOP, THINK, AND ACT

Whenever you're panicked, out of control, or facing a crisis, try using the scuba diver's motto: *Stop, think, take control, and act.* It is literally a lifesaver. It's easy to find ourselves panicked or spinning our wheels at some point during the day. If we simply stop whatever we're doing for a few minutes, think about what we should be doing, and then take the right action, we can get back on track.

Karl and I went diving in Cozumel, a beautiful island off the coast of Mexico. The diving was quite unique to us—lots of caverns and caves to explore. During one dive the back of my tank got caught while I was exiting a cave. I couldn't move. Karl was ahead of me, and I couldn't scream out to him to come back and help me. He was quite a distance away before he turned around to see where I was. I waved frantically, still unable to move. He thought I was waving to say hello and he waved back. I started to panic. I couldn't move, and I couldn't see what was hanging me up.

The more I panicked, the more air I used. That could have been very serious at the depth where we were diving. The currents were strong, and Karl had gotten too far ahead of me to be of help. It took me a few moments before I remembered to *stop* what I was doing, *think, and act.* I knew that I was caught on something. I just needed to figure out how to get unstuck. By stopping both my movements and my panic, I quickly thought about what I could be caught on and how to release it. I knew that, if necessary, I could take off my equipment and put it back on. Without anyone around to help me, this action could have saved my life. I didn't have to go that far. Just stopping and making some slight movements backward and forward released what was stuck. But I will never forget *Stop, think, take control, and act.*

Whenever you feel overwhelmed, scattered, or rushed because you have so many things to do, take a moment to stop, think, and then take the right action. You will conserve time and use your energy productively.

When Bill first read this chapter on energy conservation, he was skeptical. He admitted that he was sleeping better and felt better than before he started the program, but was doubtful that simplifying and streamlining his life would help him find a new job. Still, he decided to tackle some home improvement projects. Some trees and hedges needed trimming, the gutters needed cleaning, and the windows needed caulking. Bill found that the personal energy that he expended to put things in order also helped him emotionally. Projects that had been bothering him for a year were finished in just one week. He felt a new burst of energy and looked forward to continuing the Clarity Quest program.

CLARITY INSIGHT #6

Problems are opportunities for self-discovery and growth.

Problems offer us wonderful opportunities to expand and grow. They often force us to look at things from a different point of view and to open up the powers of our mind. In doing that, we access new ideas and insights. Problems awaken us to our inner strength and bring us in closer contact with our intuitive powers.

A PROBLEM-SOLVING EXERCISE TO ACCESS NEW INSIGHTS AND IDEAS

1. *State the problem fully and clearly.* Indicate why it's a problem. If you've lost your job, for example, the problem isn't just losing your job. Losing your job means losing your income, and that can mean going into debt, losing your house, and so on.
2. *Spend some time thinking about the problem.* Why do you

have the problem? What caused it? How do you feel about it? Can you learn anything from this problem? How can it help you grow? How is it important for your growth?

3. *Give yourself time to come up with a solution* and affirm that you will find a solution. Before going to bed, ask your dreams to help you find a solution. Practice visualization and prayer walking.

   • *Visualization.* Select three people you respect (they can be friends, family, role models, historical figures, etc.) and visualize how they would solve your problem. Ask them what would they do. How would they act? Record the answers and how you feel about them.

   • *Prayer walking.* Go for a long walk. When you begin your walk, ask for assistance in finding clear insights and a solution. On the way back, give thanks for finding a solution to your problem, even if you haven't found one yet.

4. *Record all messages that come to you in your journal.*

WEEK 5 ACTIVITIES AND EXERCISES

Take a cleansing shower each morning.

Sunday

• Take a Silence and Solitude break. Find a quiet, peaceful location and spend at least 20 minutes there alone. Be still and observe the sights around you.

• During the next three weeks, you'll begin to Lighten Your Load. You'll learn how to free up more time and energy, release unhealthy emotions, and be nourished by love so that you can bring that energy to your Quest for clarity and inspiration. With renewed strength and energy, you'll see things from a new perspective and have the mental ability to think creatively and clearly. Complete Clarity Insight #6.

- Review your calendar and map out activities for the week.
- Buy healthy foods for the week.
- Make a list of your major daily activities and see if anything can be done more efficiently. How much time could you save? What would you do with the extra time? Record in your journal.

Monday

- Visualize a smooth, productive, crisis-free day.
- Exercise.
- At the end of the workday, visualize and prepare for Tuesday. Review what must get done, what's essential, and what you can do to free up more energy.

Tuesday

- Meditate.
- Take a midday break, preferably outdoors. Practice a breathing exercise.
- Create two or three verbal affirmations. Think efficient, organized, streamlined. Add to existing affirmations and repeat 10 times daily.

Wednesday

- Visualize a smooth, productive, crisis-free day.
- Exercise.
- At the end of the workday, visualize and prepare for Thursday. Review what must get done, what's essential, and what you can do to free up more energy.

Thursday

- Meditate.
- Take a Beauty break.

Friday

- Visualize a smooth, productive, crisis-free day.
- Exercise.

Saturday

- Take an early-morning walk with your Clarity Quest buddy.
- Pick one area or room (yard, wardrobe, office) to spring clean. Choose something that will clear away the old to make way for the new and give you a real sense of accomplishment when finished.
- Complete your Progress Report and reward yourself for completing the activities this week.

PROGRESS REPORT

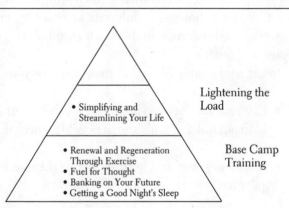

- What did you accomplish this week?
- How can you simplify your life?
- How can you become more organized and efficient?
- Make a list of what you can do to free up more time and energy.
- How are you feeling? Are you still recording your dreams?
- Have you found a location for your Quest?

Your energy during your Quest should be directed toward thinking, plain and simple. Be sure that you've done the necessary advance planning and preparation before you go. A few *minor* things can use up a *major* amount of energy.

Bob decided on a whim to take a few days off and go to the coast. He needed a little time off to recharge his batteries and to think through some work-related problems. He decided that a resort area would be a wonderful place to rest, take long walks by the sea, and recharge his batteries.

Unfortunately, his lack of advance planning hindered his efforts. He had not researched the motel that he was going to stay in. It was right along a major truck route and was extremely noisy twenty-four hours a day. He had a hard time sleeping and, as a result, had a hard time thinking the next day. He took off early in the morning to do some thinking and writing in a nearby park, but the YMCA was holding a children's summer camp right next to the area he visited. He found himself grumbling about the lack of peace and quiet.

In the next couple of weeks, make sure that you:

- Research the location and noise levels of your getaway.
- Map out walking trails and, if possible, check them out in advance.
- Check to see if any local events might interfere with your quiet time.

Record your feelings and insights in your journal.

Chapter 7

Week 6: Letting Go and Lightening Up

▓ *The office was unusually quiet when I returned to work on Wednesday. It was eerie. All of the usual morning sounds were missing—the hum of office chatter, the laughter, the exchange of greetings. I thought that I'd arrived early and checked my watch. It was 8:30. As I made my way to my desk, I noticed that several people were at their desks as well. Some were huddled in cubicles, whispering to one another. Others were on the phone, talking in hushed tones.*

I caught a few nods and smiles as I walked by. Dazed smiles that communicated shock, disbelief, sympathy, and fear. The air felt thick with emotion.

We were all in this together—at least for the next couple of weeks. Our group had been told that several jobs would be eliminated but that our managers had yet to figure out which ones. It was not knowing that was driving everyone crazy. If only they'd told us straight out, we could have used our fear constructively. The two weeks we would have to wait seemed like an eternity. I felt resentment stirring in my soul. Management hadn't taken the time to think through their next moves, and they shouldn't have said anything until they

had their act together. It seemed cruel and heartless. I felt angry and
fearful, and I wasn't sure what to do about it.

— JOURNAL ENTRY

Anger, fear, and resentment can be very powerful emotions. I refer to them as *trigger* emotions—because when they are used appropriately, they can prompt you to take action and be very constructive. Fear can warn you of danger. It can make you more cautious or motivate you to take action. Anger and resentment can give you the energy to move on. They can propel you forward and help you take positive action when you've been wronged or injured.

The problem arises when we keep these trigger emotions around and don't answer their call by taking action. Instead, we massage the problem and wallow in the emotions. When we do that, these powerful emotions can become toxic. When we continue to harbor anger, fear, and resentment, they turn destructive. If they are not eliminated in some way, they start to drain energy. A constant state of fear can paralyze you. Other emotions like anger, regret, resentment, guilt, hate, confusion, and jealousy, can weaken your immune system and keep you bound to the negative situation or person who prompted the emotion.

The management team in my colleague Stan's office decided to downsize his department because it wasn't cost-effective. Stan observed that the employees who worked through their anger and resentments were able to move forward more quickly and found other jobs. Those who wouldn't or couldn't accept the situation carried their misery and emotions with them for a longer period, affecting their ability to find new work.

There is always a feeling of great injustice when someone tells us that we're no longer valued and no longer needed. If we didn't feel anger or resentment, we wouldn't be human and wouldn't be capable of feeling other emotions such as love, joy, or happiness. We need to feel our emotions, but then we need to use them constructively.

A good friend of mine was laid off from a major bank. He and several of his peers had been invited to a meeting at which they anticipated that a new personnel policy would be announced. It was a meeting with personnel all right! The personnel folks announced that they'd all been terminated and that guards would be available to escort them back to their offices to collect their personal belongings. My friend was understandably angry and resentful toward management. His boss hadn't even attended the meeting. To my friend, all the managers became bad guys—and he was their victim.

Throughout the next year he continued to nurture his anger. He went on several interviews, but no one hired him. He later learned that his negativity had put people off. One interviewer even told him that he appeared to have a chip on his shoulder and that they had far too many qualified candidates to hire someone who was so negative. He couldn't move forward and get on with his life until he released his unhealthy emotions. He'd held on to them far too long.

Emotions become toxic when they keep us from functioning in a healthy way. When this happens, it's time to let them go. Health experts tell us that our bodies naturally strive for health, and they do so by continually cleansing themselves of waste material. If you don't cleanse yourself of toxic and unhealthy emotions, they soon become emotional baggage. Some of our emotional baggage dates back to childhood.

Think about how heavy that load is. With a lighter load, we can travel farther than we ever dreamed possible.

Some potentially unhealthy emotions that could be holding you back are:

Fear	*Resentment*
Confusion	*Hate*
Guilt	*Jealousy*
Anger	*Rejection*

If you don't take time to acknowledge and release these emotions, they eventually filter into every aspect of your life. It's far better to deal with them—to acknowledge them, feel them, take action, and release them. Not releasing unhealthy emotions binds you to the past, which keeps you from moving forward.

The goal this week is to cleanse harmful emotions from your body and mind.

WEEK 6 OBJECTIVE

To Cleanse Harmful Toxic Emotions
from Your Body and Mind

This week you'll learn:

- How to release unhealthy emotions that consume energy and keep you from moving forward
- Techniques to promote acceptance and forgiveness

ACCEPTANCE AND FORGIVENESS

We often want people to be better, kinder, or more loving than they are. One of life's hardest lessons is to accept people and situations that you cannot change. We see the person's potential, and when they don't measure up, we are disappointed.

I spent a good two-thirds of my life wishing that my sister could be more like a character in a storybook—a sister who was always loving, sweet, and supportive. A sister who was a close confidante and friend. I would read books about sisters who were best friends and wish longingly that my sister and I were closer. My sister and I are very different. She has a more scientific mind and is very analytical. I've always been more of a dreamer, lost in fantasy and poetry. We didn't always see eye to eye. We both struggled with our expectations of the other and were often very critical of each other.

Because I kept watching for whether or not she would meet my expectations, I missed out on seeing all of her wonderful traits. The minute I stopped wanting her to behave a certain way, I started to see extraordinary qualities and talents in her that I'd never noticed before. A friend who had a similar experience with his son wisely said, "You can't take a beautiful piece of jade and expect it to become the Hope diamond." It was only after he recognized that his son would never become the man he'd hoped for that he began to see the exceptional, however different, man that he was.

Often when we fall in love, we fall in love with the other person's potential. No wonder we become disappointed when reality sets in! I spent a great deal of time trying desperately to change a former boyfriend. He had so much potential, and it was frustrating to me that he wasn't realizing it. If only he'd do just a few things, he could be a happier person. If only . . . It took me a long time to realize that the other person has to *want* to change.

Now, instead of trying to change other people, I try to work on myself. The result is that I've become a much happier person. A good friend once told me, "Pam, you can only change yourself. If you try to change other people, you'll only be miserable."

Acceptance doesn't mean that we have to tolerate abhorrent situations or that we shouldn't try to change them. Sydney, a vivacious thirty-eight-year-old manager, was very angry and resentful because she'd been passed over for a promotion. She decided to wage an all-out attack. She set up meetings with senior management, wrote a letter to the CEO, and as a last resort, filed a lawsuit. She did everything she could do to change what she believed was an injustice. She used her anger and resentment to propel herself into action.

There does come a point, however, when you need to decide if a person or situation can change and how much effort you are willing to expend trying to make the change. At some point we need to accept situations and people that simply aren't going to change. Sydney fought her battle, but after doing everything she thought necessary, she needed to get on with her life.

It's possible that Sydney's managers will handle the situation differently the next time. Maybe they will, and maybe they won't. We don't always know what impact we've had, if any, until much later. We may plant a seed in someone's mind that needs time to germinate.

Sometimes life seems unfair. The wisest course is to let every situation teach us its lesson so that we grow into more compassionate and loving human beings. I love the Twelve-Step Serenity Prayer: "God, grant me the serenity to accept the things I cannot change, the courage to change the things that I can, and the wisdom to know the difference."

When we have trouble accepting others, it may be because we don't accept ourselves. Learning to forgive and accept ourselves is one of the most courageous and loving things that we can do. Many of our hurts are deeply embedded in our psyche. Think back to your childhood. How many injustices and toxic emotions are you still carrying with you? Think how heavy they are and how they weigh you down.

We want to shed these "emotional pounds," even if doing so is uncomfortable. But forgiveness can be difficult because we've never learned a formal process to release our toxic emotions.

The formula for getting rid of excess emotional baggage sounds a lot like the formula for losing weight. It is this: Eat less and exercise more. Dwell on the past less, and live more for your clarity, goals, and dreams!

THE CLEANSING PROCESS

I call the process of forgiving and shedding excess emotional baggage a cleansing process because the intent is to cleanse yourself of all harmful toxic emotions.

You need to be in the best possible shape mentally, physically, emotionally, and spiritually when facing major life changes. You want to function at your personal best and know that you are making the best possible decisions. Spa regimens around the world operate on this principle, using a "detox and cleansing" process before introducing your mind, body, and spirit to a new and healthy way of life.

To cleanse yourself of your pain and toxic emotions, it is important to:

- Acknowledge the unhealthy toxic emotion.
- Accept the situation or person that caused the emotion.
- Acknowledge what you've learned from the person or situation.
- Forgive anyone for causing you pain.
- Release the emotion.

The best way to eliminate a harmful emotion is to give it a voice. Listen to your emotion, feel it intensely, acknowledge what its purpose is in your life, and then let it go. Create a void for something better to come in.

Try the following exercise to begin the forgiving and cleansing process. If you master and embody this process, it will begin to work immediately. Think lighter. Think freedom. Remember, the goal is to reach a state of health as quickly as possible. Some people will be able to release their unhealthy emotions easily. Others might need some professional help. Do what works for you, but begin with this exercise.

A Seven-Step Acceptance and Forgiveness Exercise

1. *Focus on the situation or a person you want to forgive.* Try to see both sides of the matter, and recognize that you may only be seeing what this person did "wrong." What do others think of this person? Is she universally disliked? Has he done any good deeds?

Is she competent and productive? Should you be judging this person today? Is he capable of greatness later in life?

Remember the famous oil magnate John D. Rockefeller. His business practices were considered unscrupulous, and he was despised by many. Only later in his life did he work to set up charitable foundations, generously helping thousands of people with his money.

Is there any good in the situation you want to forgive? Can it possibly teach people lessons? Did it teach you a lesson?

Try to see the person or situation from another perspective. You might also gather viewpoints that differ from your own.

2. *What do you most dislike about the situation or person?* List all of the negatives. Spend some time and ponder your list of dislikes.

3. *Describe how this situation or person hurt you.* Examine your feelings. Write down exactly how you felt and how you feel now. Sometimes I do an exercise that I call the "Why Exercise." I learned this exercise in a College of Marin goal-setting class. It helps me uncover what I'm really feeling and why. Sometimes we mask our feelings and they become hard to access. It's difficult to cleanse unhealthy feelings until we understand them. In this exercise we'll use the example of anger. You can use this exercise for other emotions as well—fear, resentment, guilt, hate, confusion, and rejection.

The "Why Exercise"

A dear friend was transferred to a great new job in New York and invited me out to a last supper—a wonderful meal in San Francisco. He was on the phone during most of our time together and wanted to leave early to have dessert with his adult son. All understandable, but I felt angry. *Why?*

WHY ANGER?	WHY DID THAT MAKE ME ANGRY?	WHY?
I had wanted our last supper together to be special. I felt that he'd rather be doing something else.	I didn't feel special. Old reaction. I felt upset with myself. I failed to put things in perspective and look at the whole picture and be grateful for all the times he'd treated me special.	I didn't tell him how I really felt. For years I'd stuffed my feelings. Old pattern. I'd done this with many people.

Resolution. I really wasn't angry with my friend. I was angry with myself for not being honest. My friend was anxious to get on with his new life. I wanted to spend some quality time together. Of course, I never communicated this. Once I understood my anger and thought about how I could handle the situation differently in the future, my anger dissolved.

4. *Is the person doing the best she knows how to do, or did she do the best she knew how to do at the time?* While her motives might have been selfish, what would you have done in a similar situation? Try to understand the person's essence. Peel away the layers and take a look at the person's core. Don't try to make the other person be someone he is not.

The following exercise will help. I was upset with three people in my life. After doing this exercise, I realized that I could stop my anger by understanding why they behaved as they did. I could then accept them and love them for the skills they have and the joy they bring me.

Finding the "Essence" Exercise

a. What behavior upsets you?

JANICE	RON	GINA
She's very critical and judgmental. Has a history of anger and builds up a defensive wall.	Often talks about "dumping" people first, before they "dump" him.	Expects others to meet all her needs.

b. What makes them behave this way?

JANICE	RON	GINA
Grew up with an angry, abusive mother. Her mother was very critical and would cut her down in public.	Father abandoned his family. Fears abandonment.	An only child. Parents granted every wish. Was always waited on.

c. What can you learn from these people? What's good about them? Sometimes you can learn a different way of looking at and living life.

JANICE	RON	GINA
Lively mind Sense of curiosity Shares knowledge	Sense of fun Life of the party Vivacious	Adventurous Fearless

5. *Forgive yourself for not forgiving.* Remind yourself that you did the best you knew how to do as well. We can always learn from our mistakes, but don't beat yourself up because you might have done better. Use this affirmation: *I did the best I knew how to do at the time.* Say it as many times as you need to.

My parents love me very much, but they also have very high expectations. I remember receiving a report card with three As and two Bs. I was quite proud, but my parents didn't spend a lot of time praising the As. They asked instead how I could improve the Bs. They meant well and only wanted me to do my best, but later in life I became critical of myself when I didn't "get an A." It took me many years to understand that if I did the best I could do at the time, that was all that mattered. Receiving a D in a subject that was difficult for me didn't necessarily mean that I was a failure. I was trying new subjects and using new skills. If I studied only the subjects that were easy for me, I would never learn and grow.

Recently I worked for a company in Portland, Oregon. They had planned a series of broadcasts to inform their customers about some new products. The first broadcast was in January. I stepped in as a substitute producer because their first producer quit. It was a struggle to pull the program together. The client didn't return phone calls, the panelists weren't selected until three weeks before showtime, we didn't have a dry run, and the panelists and moderator were really scared. All of this showed in the quality of our broadcast.

I was determined to make the second show a success, and I did a lot of planning. I scheduled regular conference calls with all the major decision makers and managed a weekly master timeline. We had three conference calls with the panelists, and they all met in person for an all-day rehearsal and a dry run. The show was a success. The only problem was that only sixty people attended nationwide.

When we should have been basking in the glory of a very successful show, we were all disappointed because the salespeople didn't invite their customers. I was terribly disappointed. It was like planning a huge wedding and having only a few people attend. I felt that somehow it was my fault. I certainly didn't feel a lot of love for myself. It was only after a day of beating myself up and going over and over in my mind what I could have done differently, that I realized I had done the best I could possibly do.

I'm sure that the client didn't give me an A, but a B was fine with me because I'd done my best. After a while I was able to think about the things that I'd done well and to send a loving message to myself that everything was fine and that doing my best under the circumstances was enough.

6. *Write down the lessons that you learned.* Experience tells us that we learn the most valuable lessons during the most adverse conditions or relationships. What did this situation or person teach you? Write down everything you learned. Silently thank the person for teaching you this lesson.

My lesson with the company in Portland taught me that the next time I worked with this company, I should make sure that the client invited the salespeople to share responsibility for the show's concept, development, and promotion.

7. *Love is the most powerful of all emotions.* It can dissolve any hurt or injustice. Close your eyes and send a loving thought to the person. Tell them you know that they're doing the best they know how to do. Explain how they hurt you and tell them that you hope they don't harm anyone else in life. Say that you forgive them and that you're going to release them from your thoughts. You won't be bound to them any longer, and you're going to move on to a healthy and better place.

The following affirmation can be used as often as necessary to release any unhealthy emotions. I recommend saying it at least two times a day as long as you continue to feel hurt. Many people say affirmations more often because the hurt and resentment are very deep. Think of the affirmation as a cleansing process and continue using it until the toxins have been released.

I forgive you.
I send you love.
I RELEASE YOU.
I'm moving on.

One day you'll wake up and the hurt will be gone. You'll feel lighthearted and maybe even light-headed. There will be room for joy and love to enter your heart.

MOVING THROUGH THE PAIN

In addition to helping you release negative emotions, this program can help you move through the emotions associated with the loss of a person, a job, or an old way of life. It's important to set aside time to mourn your loss. When Kim lost her job, she needed to mourn not just the loss of her position but also the loss of friends, the loss of routine, and the loss of how her job made her feel.

Elisabeth Kübler-Ross, the world-renowned authority on death and dying, tells us that there are five stages that most people go through when dealing with a death—and in broader terms, the loss of a person, job, or way of life. These stages are:

1. Denial and isolation
2. Anger
3. Bargaining
4. Depression
5. Acceptance

Not everyone experiences exactly these stages, and I have found that they're not always sequential. Someone might deny a situation and then sink into heavy depression. Another person might be in the anger stage and then fall back into denial.

If you are experiencing some type of loss or think that you'll experience a sense of loss when you let go of unhealthy emotions, you might want to treat the loss as a death. Sometimes it takes a physical statement such as wearing black to remind ourselves that it's all right to feel bad. It's OK to feel pain. Give yourself permission to grieve. A death has taken place, and you may need to mourn the loss. It's all part of the cleansing process.

Some people need longer than others to mourn. The greater the loss, the harder it is to get over it. Our mind and spirit do heal in their own good time, just as our bodies do. One person's experience of loss may be like a sprained ankle; another person's may be like a broken leg. As with an injury, it's best to let yourself experience the pain so that you limit your movements and allow the healing to take place. When you don't acknowledge the physical pain, you can do more damage to your body in the long run. The same is true of emotional pain. Be gentle with yourself and take the time you need to heal. And again, get professional help if you need it.

The exercises and activities this week are designed to help you discover toxic feelings, release them, and be ready to move forward. Everyone needs a different amount of time for cleansing and healing. Some people will be able to do all the exercises by next Saturday; others will need longer. If you find that you're feeling depressed and have very low energy and want to sleep more hours than you normally sleep, that's all right. It's healthy for a while. If you're worried about being depressed or feel that you don't have the energy to do anything, you may want to seek professional help. A professional may be able to help you identify and release toxic emotions more quickly.

If you do the exercises, you will probably start to feel better. In our Western culture we often try to ignore our hurts. We carry them with us and accumulate emotional baggage. I always think of the line in a Carly Simon song, "I haven't got time for the pain." This is the week to give yourself time for the pain.

Reserve some blocks of time on your calendar this week and give yourself permission for some alone time. If you don't want to talk to certain people during the week, then don't. Take the phone off the hook. You might not be ready to tell everyone who calls what's going on in your life, or you might feel that you have to be perky or happy when you're around certain people. It's all right to screen calls right now, and it's certainly OK not to put yourself in situations that require you to be "on" or to feel something that you don't feel right now. Sometimes isolation is necessary—it helps you get in touch with your feelings faster.

Arrange for sitters, cancel appointments, call friends and let them know that you won't be available this week. This is your emotional cleansing time. Taking the time now to release and shed unhealthy emotions will help you lighten up and live your life to its fullest potential.

During a long walk on a beautiful spring evening, Linda decided it was time to let go of her anger. Her father had left her mother when she was just ten years old. He moved to another state, married again, and started a new family. Linda felt betrayed, abandoned, and rejected. She visited her father every summer but never felt part of his new family.

Linda's past anger affected her present life. She spent a great deal of time and energy thinking about her childhood. She was angry at her father, and she couldn't seem to get over it. Inevitably it affected her relationships with men, personally and professionally. She always seemed to be attracted to men who abandoned her, and with each rejection she spiraled into deeper and deeper resentment.

While she was walking, she thought about her father and tried to understand why he left. Linda remembered that her mother was not an easy woman to live with. She was angry and a manic-depressive. In denial, she refused to get help.

As she walked, Linda had a revelation. Her perception of her father's love was wrong. He'd left because he wanted a happier life but that didn't mean that he didn't love her or that she was unworthy of love. She remembered that he had fought for her custody and lost. Linda started to understand why her father had left and that he hadn't willingly abandoned her. She also realized that she, too, wanted to have a happier life and a loving relationship. Something changed. She suddenly felt lighter, more energetic, and ready to come to terms with her past and start focusing on the future.

CLARITY INSIGHT #7

*Ask the right question and your mind works
to find the right answer.*

You can focus and direct your questions to help generate new ideas and solutions. The human mind is always searching for answers and explanations. Whenever you direct a question inward, your mind goes to work to find an answer.

Asking the right question affects whether you'll discover the right answer. Think about people who ask, *"Why can't* I find a job?" or *"Why can't* I lose weight?" Their mind focuses on *why they can't* do certain things. As a result, their answers focus on why they can't do those things: they're not smart enough, not qualified enough, it's hereditary, or they've always done things the same way and can't change.

If your questions are generating answers that aren't useful, try asking different questions. For example, you might ask, *"How* can I lose weight?" or *"What* do I want in a mate?" *How can I* and *what do I need to do* questions focus on the present and the future and challenge the mind to find *new* solutions. Pay attention to where you are directing your thoughts and your questions. Do your questions dwell on the past and how you've always done something, or do they focus on the future and how you might try a new approach?

Asking the right question puts your mind to work finding the right answer. Make sure your questions are clear and direct so that your mind provides answers that are clear and understandable.

WEEK 6 ACTIVITIES AND EXERCISES

Sunday

- Take a Silence and Solitude break. Find a quiet, peaceful location and spend at least 20 minutes there alone. Be still and observe the sights around you.
- Review Insight #7 and formulate one good question to ask this week.
- Review your calendar and map out activities for the week.
- Buy healthy foods for the week, aromatic bath oils, a natural sponge, and candles. Part of the cleansing process will be to take several baths, showers, or soaks in a hot tub this week. Pick scents that induce a calm and peaceful state. If you don't want to take a bath, you can partake in another relaxing activity.
- Focus on the emotions you'd like to release this week. Write them down.
- Pick out a selection of beautiful, poignant tapes to listen to during the week. Reserve or rent a sad movie to watch on Monday.

Sunday Evening

- Run a warm bath and pour bath oil into it. Put on soft, calming music. Light candles. Slowly step into the warm water. Sit down and close your eyes for a few moments. Focus on your breathing, inhaling and exhaling slowly. Open your eyes and gently, using the sponge, squeeze water over your body and say the following prayer: *"Dear Lord, I am about to embark on a week-long cleansing program. I am ready to release any harmful toxic emotions that are weighing me down. I want to free myself. I am ready to lighten my load and discover all the exciting and new opportunities that await me."*
- Blow out the candles and express your gratitude for this week.

Monday

- Meditate 20 to 30 minutes.
- Take a midday break. Find a peaceful, quiet spot, preferably outdoors, and practice a breathing exercise.
- In the evening watch a sad movie that will make you feel deeply. When the movie is over, go to your Clarity Quest area. Write down all the emotions that surfaced. Put a star beside the emotions that are toxic. Can you think of any other emotions that might be toxic? Are they tied to a particular person or situation? Will you miss this person or situation if you release yourself of the emotions? What will you miss? If you have pictures or mementos of that person or situation, look at them. Complete Step #1 of the Acceptance and Forgiveness exercise.
- Prepare for your evening bath. Light candles. Put on soft, soothing music. Before going to bed, put on a meditation tape to help you go to sleep.

Tuesday

- Write down on a piece of loose-leaf paper all the things that you didn't like about the person or situation that evoked unhealthy emotions. Write as fast as possible.
- At twilight time take a 3- to 4-mile walk. During your walk, think about the first time you met the person or encountered the situation that caused your toxic emotions. What were your initial impressions? Spend some time with your feelings. Relive the experience in your mind. How did you feel six months later? One year later? What were the most memorable experiences? Write down on loose-leaf paper what the person or situation didn't offer you. What was missing? What needs weren't met?
- Complete Steps #2 and #3 of the Acceptance and Forgiveness exercise. Again, use loose-leaf paper.

- Prepare for your evening bath. Light candles. Put on soft, soothing music. During your bath, close your eyes and think of yourself standing under a clear mountain waterfall. Feel the water against your skin. Envision all your toxic emotions washing off your body.
- Go to bed early. Play soft, relaxing music. Drift off to sleep.

Wednesday

- Meditate 20 to 30 minutes.
- Take a midday Beauty break.
- In the evening go on a 3- to 4-mile walk, run, or hike. Think about how the person or situation helped you grow. Think about the lessons you've learned.
- Complete Steps #4 and #5 of the Acceptance and Forgiveness exercise.
- Listen to relaxing music or a meditation tape before going to sleep.

Thursday

- Go for an early-morning walk and think of all the skills that you've learned. Think about your life in perspective. What would you say about this period of life in your obituary? What would others say about you during this time? Did any of these skills contribute to your life purpose? Did you become more loving, compassionate, kind?
- Complete Step #6 of the Acceptance and Forgiveness exercise and record a master list in your journal of things you've learned, things for which you are grateful, and lessons you have learned. How did this experience contribute to your growth? List all the people you'll miss if you're moving on. Put stars by the ones with whom you want to stay in touch.
- Prepare for your evening bath. Light candles. Put on soft, soothing music. During your bath, close your eyes and feel

the toxic emotions coming to the surface of your skin. Wash them off with your sponge. When you empty the bath, think of them washing down the drain. Listen to relaxing music or a meditation tape before drifting off to sleep.

Friday

- Meditate 20 to 30 minutes.
- Take a midday break. Find a peaceful, quiet location, preferably outdoors. Are you ready to release your unhealthy emotions? If not, try the "Why Exercise" to see what you're still hanging on to and why.
- Exercise.
- Complete Step #7 of the Acceptance and Forgiveness exercise. Make up your own affirmations. Light candles, lower the lights, and repeat the affirmations as many times as needed.
- Go to bed early and use Muscle Relaxation Exercise #3 before retiring (see Chapter 2).

  Imagine a golden ball of white light above your head. As you inhale, imagine the light coming into your body. Visualize the light burning brightly. As you relax each part of your body, see the light burning away any harmful toxic emotions.

Saturday

- Gather all the loose-leaf papers that you've created this week. Select a bright, bold outfit to wear.
- Before leaving home, burn the loose-leaf papers and put the ashes into a small jar.
- *Release Ceremony/Funeral Service*

  Find a beautiful, isolated, sacred place—a beach, woods, mountaintop, or some other place that feels safe. Think of where you'd scatter the ashes of a loved one. When you get to the sacred destination, say the following: *"I'm here today to release the past and to release any emotions that were becoming toxic to my body, mind, or soul.*

There will be some things that I will miss. But in my heart I know that I can carry all the good that came from this situation or person. This will stay with me forever."

Scatter the ashes slowly. As you do so, think of all the negative things about this situation or person. Things that you gladly release. Once all the ashes are scattered, think of all the positive things that will stay in your heart forever. Treasured memories. Be grateful for the lessons you learned and the skills you acquired. Say to yourself and the universe: *"I release my past. I am free to move on. I treasure all the people and skills and lessons that I learned. I carry them in my heart. My experiences have helped to make me the person that I have become. I am ready to continue my growth. I am free to move on. My future is calling!"*

• Complete your Progress Report.

PROGRESS REPORT

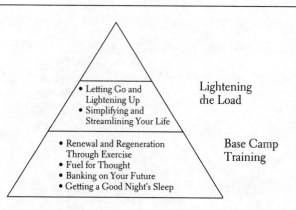

- Letting Go and Lightening Up
- Simplifying and Streamlining Your Life

Lightening the Load

- Renewal and Regeneration Through Exercise
- Fuel for Thought
- Banking on Your Future
- Getting a Good Night's Sleep

Base Camp Training

• What did you accomplish this week?
• Were you able to release your toxic emotions? If not, why?
• Do you feel lighter, healthier, and ready to continue your journey?

- Have you made all the necessary arrangements to take time off for your Quest? Found a location? Made reservations? Scheduled time away from work? Identified people to pick up the paper and mail, take care of your children, pets, or house?

Record your answers in your journal.

Chapter 8

Week 7: High-Power Energetics

▤ *This journey we are on is not always an easy one. There are many paths that can be taken, and many obstacles to challenge us. How refreshing it is to be joined along the way—to share one's travels, adventures, hopes, and dreams with another.*

I am so grateful that we were able to share the same path for a while, to walk side by side. You opened my heart and expanded my world.

I think about you from time to time and continue to feel your love. It is stored in my heart and I draw on it to give me energy. It was never wasted. Nor did it go away. It sustains me on days when I'm too weary or too tired to think about going further.

Perhaps our paths will cross again in this lifetime. Perhaps another. In the meantime, know that my love will always be with you, as yours is with me. Take care of yourself and be happy.

—A LOVE LETTER

Take a moment to think of someone whom you love dearly. How do you feel when you think about him? How do you feel when you're around that person? Can you feel her love for you?

Can you feel your love in return? The love you feel is pure energy and can be very powerful.

Love is the most powerful form of energy that exists. It can transform us in an instant and give us the energy we need to perform any feat imaginable.

You can be nourished by three types of love: divine love, love for yourself, and love for others. All love can dissolve fears, wipe out negative emotions, quiet troublesome thoughts, and bring inner serenity. Remember the scene in the *Wizard of Oz* when Dorothy throws water on the wicked witch and the witch begins to melt away? The same thing can happen with love. You can melt away any fears or negative thoughts and even negative people when you throw love on them.

I used to visit a ninety-seven-year-old man in a rest home. He was a kind and gentle soul. He radiated love and always had a kind word for everyone. I would often look into his sparkling blue eyes and feel pure love. I met Sepp through a volunteer program called LITA, Love Is The Answer. The program allows pets and their owners to visit nursing home residents once a week. Sepp was a delightful person. He always went out of his way to help people, saying kind words to them and sending them love. He often called me at home right after I visited to thank me for spending time with him. He would always end the call with the words "Darling, I love you." What sweet, beautiful words. My heart would soar.

After several visits to the nursing home, I began contrasting Sepp's behavior with that of his neighbors. Several of them had turned bitter and never missed a chance to express their worries, fears, and hatred. Sepp, on the other hand, exuded love, good health, and good cheer. People stayed away from the bitter, angry people. Even some of the nurses avoided them. But Sepp always had a flock of people around him. He gave love freely. The more he gave, the more he got back. It was a simple, valuable lesson for me.

The more I visited Sepp, the more I realized that he not only loved others but also loved himself. His neighbors desperately wanted love, but they didn't love themselves and had a very hard time loving others. They were like wilted plants that desperately needed nourishment. One lady in particular was very hard on herself. In her own eyes she could do nothing right. She constantly criticized herself and talked about how selfish she was.

Sepp's love for himself and others gave him great reserves of energy, and he was able to go to that reservoir any time that he wanted. Think of how much energy we spend doubting ourselves, being hard on ourselves, blaming ourselves, and feeling guilty for our actions. Loving and nurturing ourselves helps us stockpile reserves of love and energy. Ironically, once we start giving love to ourselves and others, we receive it back multiplied.

The goal this week is to learn how to be nourished by the three types of love and to experience inner serenity. Love is the soul's most essential nutrient. Just as your body needs fuel to keep functioning and stay healthy, your soul needs love nourishment to keep it healthy and vibrant.

WEEK 7 OBJECTIVE

To Be Nourished by Three Types of Love:
Divine Love, Love for Yourself, and Love for Others

This week you'll learn:

- ✔ How love can dissolve fears, quiet oppressive thoughts, and provide inner security
- ✔ Techniques to practice loving yourself and others
- ✔ How to connect with the Divine

LOVING YOURSELF

You can love and nurture yourself in many ways. Review the list you made in Chapter 3 of things that make you feel special and good. Whenever you do something special for yourself, do it with love. If you have a hard time feeling love, think about someone you love. The feeling of love begins to radiate from your soul. Now turn it inward. Feel that love and say to yourself, "*I love myself. I am a beautiful, special person, and I deserve to be loved.*"

Loving yourself sometimes means being more accepting of yourself. We've all made mistakes and felt disappointed in ourselves from time to time. We are here to learn from our mistakes. Don't dwell on them. Remember that you did the best you knew how to do at the time. Think about what you learned and what you could do differently the next time. A parent doesn't stop loving a child just because the child makes a mistake. And a child needs to make many mistakes in order to learn and grow.

I remember feeling the great power of parental love after running into the side of my father's car while driving my mother's car. I was sixteen years old and had just gotten my driver's license. My mother needed a few items at the store and I volunteered to go. It was one of the first times I'd driven alone. What a wonderful feeling of freedom! I didn't check the speedometer, but it felt great to be cruising down the city streets. I was probably going a little fast when I came back home, turned into the driveway, and discovered that my father's car was parked on the left-hand side of the garage. I hadn't looked. I had simply sped down the block, made a beautiful turn into the driveway, and sideswiped my father's car.

The sound of metal scratching metal is never pretty. I managed to damage both cars and felt miserable. I'd been careless, and I feared that my new wings would be clipped for sure. I braced myself and went into the house to tell my father, fearing his recrimination. He was my mentor and role model. I hated to disappoint him.

Before I finished telling him about the accident, I burst into tears. He looked at me stoically and didn't say a word. I'm sure he was quite angry, but he didn't say anything. I went to my room and softly closed the door. He knocked on it a few minutes later. I thought that if there were ever a time for punishment, this would be it.

He looked at me with eyes filled with love and said that if I'd learned a lesson from this accident, that's what mattered the most. I wasn't hurt, the cars could be repaired, and if this accident would help to slow me down and prevent me from driving carelessly in the future, it would be well worth it.

Of course, I'd learned a lesson. I had learned not only about being careless and speeding but also about the power of unconditional love. Treat yourself the same way a loving parent would treat a child.

Love is a very powerful emotion. When we love ourselves, we can literally dissolve our fears, anxieties, and tensions.

I know many people who constantly put themselves down. They openly criticize themselves with words like "I'm so stupid. I'm so clumsy. I can't do anything right. I'm not attractive enough. I always manage to screw things up. I'm overweight. My hair is always a mess." Negative chatter can be very damaging because your subconscious believes what you tell it. Your subconscious doesn't argue with you; it just absorbs everything you say. The next time you hear yourself saying something negative about yourself, stop. Send yourself love and replace the sentence with a loving message, something like *"I love myself, and I'm doing the best, looking the best, and being the best that I know how to be and do right now."*

LOVING OTHERS

When you love yourself, loving others is much easier. One of my favorite affirmations is *"I do one loving gesture daily."* It's fun to think about what that one loving gesture will be. I think first of family and close friends. What little thing can I do to demonstrate my love for them? My parents always appreciate it when I call them. But when I take the time to go buy a pretty card and write a thoughtful note, I'm filled with love and happiness, and I'm sure they appreciate that even more. Jan's co-worker was going through a tough time, so she brought her a colorful bouquet of flowers with a note. She took another friend to lunch one day when she was feeling down. Jerry loves to prepare wonderful meals for his wife. The aromas greet her when she gets home from a stressful day, and he knows that she appreciates that.

My husband tells me how much he appreciates the little cards I leave for him in his briefcase. They make him smile in the middle of a stressful meeting.

One time when I was leaving town, I taped a card outside on the door leading from the garage to the house. I printed his name boldly on the card to make sure he didn't miss it. The card instructed him to go to the CD player. Nicely wrapped was a new Rod Stewart tape and a card with instructions telling him to play "Have I Told You Lately That I Love You?" Then I had him proceed to the refrigerator. There he found a bottle of champagne decorated with a beautiful ribbon. Another card instructed him to have a glass of champagne and look for a package upstairs in his dresser. My final wrapped package included two tickets to a hockey game he wanted to see but was sold out.

I had so much fun thinking about all the things that he loves and showing him with a few kind gestures how much I loved him.

Kind gestures can be as simple as calling someone up and telling him that you love him and value his friendship. It's easy to get caught up in work and be concerned with your own troubles — but the magic of love is that when you give it away, you get it back multiplied.

My mother buys little holiday gifts for close friends and family throughout the year. I know it brings her great joy just to think about the special things that she can give to other people. At Christmas she bakes special cookies and candies for her neighbors and delivers pies to friends for special occasions.

Small, simple gestures can mean a great deal. Karl gets up early on weekends and greets me with a steaming cup of coffee in bed. His parents send us cards and checks on Valentine's Day and our anniversary and tell us to go out and celebrate on them! My friend

Carolyn prepared a wonderful picnic for my birthday, and we celebrated at the beach. My good friend Joe goes out of his way to send special cards and gifts throughout the year. One time he sent twenty beautiful blank greeting cards from his favorite card shops and museums in New York, and a sheet of beautiful stamps. They were from the Georgia O'Keeffe collection with the famous quote "Nobody sees a flower, really—it is so small—we haven't time, and to see takes time, like to have a friend takes time."

The book *A Course in Miracles*, a self-study program in spiritual psychology, tells us that everything we do is either love or a call for love. Even the crankiest, meanest person you meet is really just asking for love. Karl and I were both in our late thirties when we married. It was Karl's first marriage and my second. Neither of us had children, but we both had old male dogs. Bob, my beautiful golden retriever, had been with me since he was a puppy. He is a loving, gentle dog who greets all strangers with a wagging tail. We joke that if a burglar ever came to the door, Bob would wag his tail and invite the guy in.

Karl's dog, Snowball, is a beautiful American Eskimo and was given away twice as a puppy. He barked incessantly and showed his fangs to everyone except Karl. The first time our dogs met, Snowball tried to go for Bob's jugular. Luckily, Bob was the older, larger dog and soon became the alpha dog.

It was a trying first six months for all of us. I was used to petting Bob a lot and giving him many hugs during the day. When I tried to pet Snowball, he showed his fangs and tried to bite me. He actually did bite me one night when Karl was away. I called dog obedience schools and pleaded with them to give me guidance. They advised me that I couldn't do much with an older dog. The only thing I could do, they said, was to show him that I was the boss. One trainer even recommended violence. She suggested that I pick him up and throw him against the wall, just to show him who was the boss.

For the next three months Snowball and I had quite a power struggle. I wasn't willing to resort to violence, and I didn't want to ask Karl to give up his dog. Karl was quite attached to Snowball, and I couldn't, wouldn't ask him to give him up. Given Snowball's past, Karl had been quite successful with him. Love for animals is as strong a love as any human bond that I've experienced. But what was I to do about Snowball?

Bob showed me the solution. Bob is such a loving dog that even though Snowball often snarled and tried to attack him, Bob really cared for Snowball. When I put Snowball outside, Bob would whine until I let him in. Whenever Snowball was in trouble, Bob would go up to him and whine. Bob was so loving that Snowball accepted him in about a month.

I decided to try it out. Rather than snapping at Snowball and sending him off to obedience school, I tried to be more loving toward him. I talked to him in a calm voice and praised him often. I sent him loving thoughts and I gave him his space. I stopped trying to get him to behave like Bob. It was only a short time before he let me stroke him while I praised him.

A good friend once told me that some people need the love coaxed out of them. This was certainly true of Snowball. He turned out to be a real pushover who desperately wanted love and responded to it with affection. He learned faster through love than he had with harsh words and commands.

I'm the same way. I've always responded to love and people who have believed in me. I've opened up, blossomed, and learned much faster. Harsh words make me shut down, close up, and build defenses to protect myself.

Try sending loving thoughts to a complete stranger. Have you ever told a salesclerk how helpful she was or how wonderfully she handled a situation? Those who are receptive just beam, and you know that you've added a sparkle to their day. People who aren't as receptive probably need the love coaxed out of them. Have you ever had a stranger get angry at you and diffused their anger with love?

Any kindness toward others is a form of love. And the more love you spread, the more fears you dissolve. Unnecessary fears deplete,

Learn every skill.

waste, and block our energy. They leave us in an unhealthy state, unable to move forward or to grow.

RECEIVING LOVE

By showing love to yourself, you open up to receive love from others. Being able to receive love typically means that you value yourself and know that you are worthy. A close friend of mine says that she has a hard time receiving. She gives love to others easily but has a hard time accepting it in return. She struggles with being able to receive partly because she doesn't feel worthy and partly because she doesn't want to relinquish control. It is very vulnerable to open yourself up to receive love. But when you do so, others open their hearts as well.

Think about how happy you are when you do something loving for others. My good friend Irene has mastered the art of showing other people how much she appreciates them. She sends beautiful cards and little gifts frequently to many of her close friends. During the holidays she buys her employees gifts and takes them out for a special celebration. Once when I was staying at her house, she had flowers and a little present wrapped for me in the guest room. Giving love to someone who doesn't receive the gift stops the flow. When you don't receive love from others, you rob them of the joy of giving.

It's an interesting formula: The more you give, the more you receive. And the more you receive, the more you give. Receiving your own love opens the door to receiving love from others.

LOVE POWER

Some people use sheer *will*power to get through a challenging situation, survive a personal crisis, or accomplish goals. Their determination and persistence give them the energy to accomplish what they set out to do. I like to draw on *love* power to help me through the tough times, deal with difficult people, or face new challenges. Love power can transform any relationship or situation.

I once interviewed for a job in a large Fortune 500 company. I'd been told that I would have to talk to ten people in the course of a day, plus have lunch with the assistant vice president and the vice president of the department. It sounded intimidating. I was excited and nervous and fearful, all at the same time.

I didn't actually feel qualified for the job. It was a stretch for me, and I was worried that I wasn't quite good enough. I wanted the job, but I feared someone would discover that I wasn't up to it. That made me extremely nervous, and I soon started worrying that I'd sabotage my own chances.

Somehow I had to turn my fear into a state of love. I researched the company, researched the department, and still felt inadequate and fearful. The only thing that saved me was to draw on love power. I sent loving thoughts to all ten people and also to the vice president and the assistant vice president, even though I'd never met them. I closed my eyes and mentally said, *"Right action will take place for the highest good of all concerned."* I knew that if I could come from a place of love, not fear, I could perform at my best. If they still didn't like me or didn't think I was qualified, that would be all right. It would mean that the job wasn't the right one for me. I just wanted to give it my best shot. I got the job!

Sandra practiced sending love to a man she didn't respect or trust. She had stopped her car at a busy intersection near her house. Several cars were stopped in front of her at the light, and after a couple of minutes she released her foot from the brake. Her car slowly rolled into a truck in front of her. She wasn't on a hill, but there must have been a slight incline for her to roll forward. Her bumper lightly tapped the bumper in front of her.

The driver got out of his truck to check for damage, so she got out to look as well. No sign of damage, not even a scratch. Still, he asked for her name and number and she willingly gave it to him. Immediately after she'd given him the information, he told her that he'd recently been in an accident and that the other driver had no insurance. A little voice inside her told her not to trust this man, but she paid no heed. There were plenty of witnesses around, but she didn't get their names.

The next day the driver of the truck left a message on her answering machine asking for the name of her insurance company because his neck felt out of whack and he knew that he'd have to see a doctor. Sandra had a hard time believing that he could have sustained any injuries from the encounter, and she was angry. This person was trying to take advantage of the system and at her expense. She tossed and turned throughout the night. The next day she decided to draw on love power. She sent him loving messages and explained that if he truly believed she'd harmed him, he should let her know. If not, she asked him to accept her love and told him not to do damage to others. She continued her mental love power messages to him for three days and never heard from him again.

Sometimes I draw on love power before an important meeting or before making a cold call. I close my eyes for a few moments and send loving thoughts to everyone I'm going to encounter. If I have a hard time feeling love, I think about someone whom I love dearly. When I think about that person, I can feel his love. I surround myself with love and pretend that I'm taking a shower with love flowing over me. Once I'm completely covered with love, I send it to others.

Love is very potent, and even a little bit goes a long way.

UNCONDITIONAL LOVE AND ROMANTIC LOVE

Some people confuse all love with romantic love. In the early blush of a relationship, romantic love feels wonderful. You feel light-headed and blissful, and the whole thing is just intoxicating.

Romantic love is an important form of love, but it's even better when it turns into unconditional love. When you first fall in love with someone, you see her wonderful potential but sometimes miss the warts, flaws, and shortcomings. You don't always see the whole person. When the first blush of romance wears off a bit, sometimes we see a little more clearly and become disappointed. It's more difficult to accept another person when she doesn't measure up to our expectations.

For romantic love to grow, you need to see the whole person and love the whole person. When you love someone unconditionally, you accept him and love him just as he is. Unconditional love is unselfish love. You think of what's best for the other person, not necessarily for yourself. Sometimes this means letting him go. Some people selfishly cling to their illusions about other people because they're fearful of being alone. If you always wish the best for others, you'll never be alone.

DIVINE LOVE

Divine energy is the most powerful because it is pure love—pure, unconditional love. The best way to restore and replenish your energy is to connect with the Divine as you understand it—God, Buddha, Christ, Allah. Imagine plugging into a higher voltage of pure electricity, pure power, pure love that is always there and always available to you. No matter what your spiritual beliefs, you will feel a great surge of energy when you can tap into this higher power.

There are many places that you can feel this love, even if you're a nonbeliever.

LOVE IN NATURE AND IN ALL THINGS OF BEAUTY

When Linda is out walking in nature, she can't help feeling a connection to the Divine. She feels pure love, and a feeling of tranquillity washes over her soul. It sometimes takes her awhile to slow down and allow the love and beauty to enter her soul.

The four seasons of the year give us many opportunities to feel love. In springtime everything seems to be a soft green, bursting with life. In summer the days are long and warm and carefree. In fall the colors are vibrant and fiery and the air is crisp and refreshing. Winter brings its stillness, whiteness, and peace.

There is a Divine plan and a Divine love for all living things. All things of beauty are divinely inspired. When you look at something beautiful, don't you feel a soul connection with something greater? It might be a beautiful place, a beautiful piece of art, or a beautiful piece of music. No language is required for us to appreciate these things.

If you take time to see the beauty in others and in life, you will feel surrounded by love. If you incorporate beauty into your life, you are actually incorporating love into your life. Joan loves to grow beautiful flowers in her backyard. It makes her happy just to look out the window at them. She also loves to have beautiful pieces of artwork in her house and to play beautiful music. She knows these things as love and enjoys them to the fullest. Alexandra Stoddard wrote a loving and inspirational book called *Living a Beautiful Life*. It is filled with great tips on making everyday activities as beautiful and pleasurable as possible.

LOVE IN PLACES OF WORSHIP

While I was growing up, I went to church every Sunday. Then after college I just stopped going to church. I moved to a large city and found a multitude of other activities on Sundays. It seemed that everything competed with church services.

When my first marriage was failing, I started exploring various churches and spiritual practices. I found great comfort and solace in just sitting in a church. I had first discovered the comfort of this loving energy while traveling through Europe one summer. It was so hot that sometimes we would duck into a cathedral just to cool down and rest our poor swollen feet. It was so delightful. Sitting quietly in a darkened church for a few moments and just watching the candles flicker was very restorative.

The loving energy remains in churches after worship services are over, and a church that practices love leaves you feeling recharged. In A Guide to Confident Living, Norman Vincent Peale talks about a doctor who prescribed church services to a patient. He recommended going to church one day a week for three months because the mood and atmosphere contained real healing power. You don't even have to listen to the sermons if you don't want to. Just sit and be still. The love will permeate your soul.

A certain magic also occurs when you're in the presence of others who are connecting with the Divine. I always remember that beautiful passage in the Bible about "whenever two or more are gathered in my name, there is love." Reading spiritual passages and books can also be very nourishing to your soul.

In times of crisis we often allow ourselves to feel vulnerable. We may feel more deeply that something is missing and be more willing to explore alternatives than we are in good times. Use this time to your advantage, and open up to your connection with the Divine.

LOVE IN PRAYER

Prayer is another wonderful way to connect with more love, and it can also be a great comfort to our souls. Prayer is like having an open line to the Divine anytime that you want. You can talk about anything or ask for any assistance you want. God is love, and love is energy. In *Healing Words*, Dr. Larry Dossey describes the power of prayer to heal and notes scientific experiments showing that prayer positively affects high blood pressure, wounds, heart attacks, headaches, and anxiety.

When I was a little girl, I would kneel beside my bed at night, fold my hands, close my eyes, and begin praying: "Now I lay me down to sleep, I pray the Lord my soul to keep. If I should die before I wake, I pray the Lord my soul to take. God Bless Mom and Dad and Grandpa and Grandma, even Debbie and Rhonda. Amen." It was a simple prayer, but it was tremendously comforting. When we pray, we open ourselves to receive love, to give love, and to give thanks.

Whenever you want to connect with Divine Love, try a simple prayer. I can almost guarantee that you'll feel tranquillity and peace in your soul.

After reading this chapter, Dana looked in the phone book and located a church near her apartment. She wasn't Catholic, but she decided to go to evening mass, sit in the back of the church, and quietly observe the service. During a moving guitar solo she thought about everyone she'd loved during her life and how grateful she was to experience their love. She made a list of all these people when she got home, and wrote down what their love had meant to her. Dana decided to contact all of them during the week and let them know how much she appreciated them. She called some people, sent cards to others, and took her parents and her boyfriend out to dinner. She felt an incredible outpouring of love and support from everyone she contacted and planned to bring this energy with her to her Quest for guidance and inspiration.

CLARITY INSIGHT #8

Physical movement helps to stimulate the imagination.

Fears and incessant mental chatter keep us from thinking clearly. Our thoughts are scattered, and it's hard to focus and concentrate.

If you're stuck on a problem or want to think more clearly about a particular issue, stand up and start moving. A good brisk walk or workout will increase your circulation and deliver more blood and oxygen to your brain. Once you start moving, your body releases chemicals in the brain that alleviate tension and stress. You become clearly focused and can come up with more creative solutions.

Before you begin your walk or workout, think about the problem you'd like to solve. Define it clearly, then start moving. Don't think about the problem. Your mind will gradually start working through the issue. Once you calm down the chatter and become more focused, you can think clearly and creatively.

WEEK 7 ACTIVITIES AND EXERCISES

Remember to take a cleansing shower each morning.
Sunday

- Take a Silence and Solitude break. Find a quiet, peaceful location and spend at least 20 minutes there alone. Be still and observe the sights around you.
- Try practicing Clarity Insight #8 this week.
- Review your calendar and map out activities for the week.
- Buy healthy foods for the week.
- Go to a place of worship. Sit quietly and feel the energy.
- Review the list of Things That Make You Feel Good in

Chapter 3. Pick one activity to do for yourself this week and one to do for someone else.

- Confirm all plans and reservations for your Clarity Quest. Read "A Few Tips Before You Go on Your Quest," page 188.

Monday

- Meditate.
- Exercise.
- Create two or three loving verbal affirmations. Think about loving yourself and others. Add to your affirmations and repeat 10 times daily.

Tuesday

- Take a midday break, preferably outdoors. Practice a breathing exercise.
- Practice love power. Spend 5 minutes sending someone love.

Wednesday

- Meditate.
- Take a walk with your Clarity Quest buddy.

Thursday

- Take a Beauty break. Find a place that nourishes your soul.
- Complete your Progress Report and reward yourself for completing Part Two. Take some time to reflect on what you've accomplished and how much more energetic you're feeling.

Friday

- Meditate.
- Exercise.
- Pack and prepare for your Clarity Quest.
- Go to bed early. Play relaxing music or a meditation tape.

PROGRESS REPORT

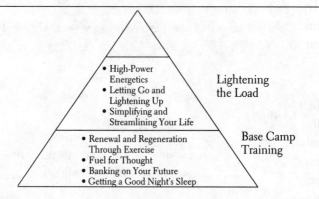

- What did you accomplish this week?
- Make a list of everything that nourishes your soul. How can you experience more love in your life?
- How are you feeling—mentally, emotionally, physically, and spiritually?
- Think about what you'd like to accomplish during your Quest. What would you like clarity on?

Record your feelings and insights in your journal.

A FEW TIPS BEFORE YOU GO ON YOUR QUEST

1. *Plan meals.* Review Chapter 4, "Fuel for Thought," and make sure that all the foods you eat during the week are healthy and energize you. Don't eat food that leaves you feeling sluggish.

2. *Let important people know that you're going away for a few days and can't be reached.* Leave a message on your answering machine telling callers that you won't be checking messages until you return.

3. *Incorporate lots of Nature and Beauty breaks into your Quest.* Try to spend as much time as you can outdoors in natural, peaceful settings. Avoid man-made sounds as much as possible. Draw on nature for inspiration.

4. *Be willing to accept and listen to your inner guidance.* The best way to start doing this is to be truthful with yourself. During the week you'll be working on a number of exercises that require total honesty. Don't gloss over things or say things just because others might expect you to do so. This is your life, not your parents', your spouse's, or your friends' lives. As you contemplate what actions to take, trust your own judgment. Take enough time during the exercises to ask yourself, "Is this what I really want? Is this how I really feel?"

5. *Record all your exercises in your journal.* You are making a blueprint for your future and want an easy reference.

6. *Review Clarity Insights.* If you're looking for the solution to a problem, try the visualization or prayer walking exercise (Insight #6). If you've been asking a question and haven't received a clear answer, try asking a different question (Insight #7). Remember that asking the right question will put your mind at work to find the right answer. Make sure all your questions are clear and direct so that your mind will provide answers that are clear and understandable. If you're having a hard time making a decision during the week, review Clarity Insight #4 and complete the exercise.

7. *Take lots of walks and continue to exercise during the week.* Ideas have a way of popping into your mind when you are moving. A stagnant mind is like stagnant water. There is no movement or flow. If you're having a hard time concentrating or get stuck, get up and get moving!

8. *Make a list of what you should bring.* Packing will go faster and you'll avoid forgetting that one special item that might make your adventure more pleasant. Include exercise clothes, walking shoes, healthy foods, inspirational books, music and meditation tapes, aromatic bath oils, and candles. Make sure you leave all your work at home.

9. *Release all thoughts and feelings that could prevent you from realizing your dreams.* Is there any person, emotion, or belief that is preventing you from reaching your goals? Are you willing to release that person, emotion, or belief so that you can have a more joyful and satisfying life? Before you begin your Quest, consider having a special ceremony to release fears, old beliefs, and blockages.

Find a sacred, beautiful place. Close your eyes and take 10 to 20 slow, deep, abdominal breaths. Imagine each breath filling your body with light. Imagine each exhalation removing any blockages. Say to yourself and the Universe: "*I am here today to release all people, emotions, and beliefs that could prevent me from achieving my potential. I'm grateful for the skills and lessons that I've learned from them. But I'm now ready to move forward. I release my past. I am free to realize my dreams. My future is bright with possibilities.*"

10. *Be committed to taking action.* Many people have great ideas and clear ideas, but follow-through is what often makes the difference between failure and success.

Part Three

REACHING
THE
SUMMIT

Chapter 9

Week 8: Clarity Quest: The Guided Week-Long Sabbatical

▓ *So often I yearn to just get away. To escape the turbulent waters of my life, the confusion, the conflict, the pain. I seek a place where I can be still and reflect and see clearly into the depths of my soul.*

— JOURNAL ENTRY

Congratulations! It's time to pack your bags and embark on a wonderful journey of self-discovery and personal fulfillment. This is a week to revitalize, take stock, and find new meaning and direction in your life.

On a deep level we know the type of work, relationships, and life that will make us feel alive, happy, and gratified. This week you will access that wisdom as you spend time in beautiful, tranquil places and engage in daily activities and exercises to reveal a clear vision of who you are and what you want from your job and your life. You will also identify the steps you need to take to make your dream a reality.

With the renewed strength and energy you've gained over the past seven weeks, you will be able to think deeply, creatively, and clearly and see your life from a new perspective.

WEEK 8 OBJECTIVE

To Develop a Clear Vision of What You Want from
Your Life and Livelihood and Create a Plan to Get It

This week you'll:

- Identify your greatest strengths and powers
- Clarify what you really want
- Design a life in harmony with your core values
- Set specific and clear goals to get what you want
- Create a visualization and action plan to keep you focused
  and on target

This chapter organizes your Quest into a focused, structured adventure. Think of it as a traveler's guide. Each day's plan is designed to help you get the most out of that day. Each exercise has a suggested time limit, and the schedule includes several breaks so that you can relax and recharge.

I suggest that you review each day's plan in advance and personalize it to fit your needs. There are five days of planned activities and exercises. You might want to add other activities to make your adventure more enjoyable—local sightseeing, watching the stars at night, napping, exercising, or pampering yourself with a massage or body treatment.

One woman decided to take her writing and visioning exercises with her on the long hikes she would take during the week and do them out in nature. She mapped out a scenic trail to take each day, packed a picnic lunch and snacks, and brought along plenty of water and layered clothing. She hiked at a leisurely pace and discovered several beautiful areas where she could work on her exercises. Jack decided to spend his week in Paris. He felt so alive in Paris and discovered charming cafés, museums, and parks to work on his exercises. He felt both rejuvenated and renewed when he returned home.

You have the power to manifest your dreams this week! Take time to think carefully about what you want and pay special attention to your thoughts and words. Make sure that they are positive and focused on the good that you want to create. Have a wonderful Quest!

DAY 1 ACTIVITIES AND EXERCISES

Carry your notebook and pen with you this week, and keep them next to your bed at night. Be prepared to record all flashes of inspiration and insight.

Activities

- Take an early-morning walk. Reflect on the beginning of this new day and the beginning of your new life. Think about everything you've learned during the past seven weeks and what you would like to accomplish this week.
- Find a location that's peaceful and quiet, and complete Exercise #1, "What Do You Want to Accomplish?" *Suggested time: 1–1½ hours*
- Read "Identifying What You Naturally Do Well," and complete Exercises #2–5. Read "Discovering What Motivates You," and complete Exercises #6–11. *Suggested time: 2–3 hours*
- Take a Silence and Solitude break. Be still and listen to the sounds around you.
- Read "Identifying Your Greatest Strengths and Power," and complete Exercises #12–19. *Suggested time: 2 hours*
- After dinner, take a beautiful evening walk. Breathe slowly, observe all things of beauty, and reflect on your greatest strengths.
- Prepare for an evening bath or shower. Light candles. Put on soft, soothing music. Use a muscle relaxation exercise to relax all the muscles in your body. Think about your

strengths and all the wonderful things that make you unique. Be grateful.

- Go to bed early. Before going to sleep, ask your dreams for clear guidance and direction. Listen to relaxing music or a meditation tape before drifting off to sleep.

Exercises

Exercise #1: What Do You Want to Accomplish?

Find a comfortable sitting position. Remember to keep your spine straight to allow a good flow of energy.

1. Close your eyes and begin breathing slowly and calmly. Take 10 to 20 slow, deep breaths. Be aware of your breath moving in and out. As you inhale, say, "I receive." As you exhale, say, "I let go." Let go of any tension or pain in your body. Exhale all tension until you feel calm and peaceful.

2. Relax your whole body. Using the muscle relaxation technique, travel through your body, relaxing each area. Imagine a flame of white light moving through you, removing all impurities and tensions. Feel yourself growing serene and calm.

3. Imagine roots in the bottom of your feet. As you continue breathing, imagine them slowly going down into the earth.

4. Ask your higher self for guidance and direction during your Quest. Express gratitude for a healthier and stronger body and for a clear and alert mind. Give thanks for this time alone in a beautiful place and for the opportunity to be quiet and still and to think and hear clearly.

5. Focus on what you want to accomplish this week. What do you really want in life? Who do you want to become? Imagine a door in front of you. When you step through the door, enter the new life you want to create. Picture it as clearly as possible. What do you look like? How do you feel? What new

qualities do you have? What positive changes do you want to create in your life? Use all of your senses. If any negative thoughts surface, imagine sweeping them away with a broom. If you're not clear, ask for further insight and clarification this week.

6. When you feel calm and relaxed and are ready, open your eyes. Take a few moments to reorient yourself. Take some deep breaths and stretch.

7. Record your visualization in your journal.

Identifying What You Naturally Do Well

What you do naturally is often what you do best. It is what distinguishes you as an individual and what makes you unique. Each of us has special talents, qualities, and skills. No two great composers and artists have produced the same piece of music or art. No two fingerprints are the same, and no two voices are identical.

You were born with these special talents, skills and qualities—or have a high aptitude for them. You do these things naturally, and in doing them, you express your greatest level of competence.

WHAT YOU DO WELL

What Makes You Special and Unique
Natural Talents, Special Qualities, and Skills

NATIVE/ INHERENT TALENT	PERSONALITY/ SPECIAL QUALITIES	ACQUIRED SKILLS/ EXPERTISE
Athletic	Optimistic	Sales and marketing
Artistic	Energetic	Communications
Musical	Honest	Organization
Intellectual	Determined	Planning
Analytical	Charming	Crafts/Trades

The following exercises are designed to reveal your unique talents, qualities, and skills. If you've done a variation on these exercises before, do them again. With your heightened awareness, you will discover some new things about yourself. Remember to think positively.

Exercise #2

List natural talents, qualities, and skills that you discovered and expressed at various times in life. Probing into your past will help you uncover talents that you've buried or haven't used in a while.

Natural Talents, Qualities and Skills

Grade School:

High School:

College:

Young Adult:

Adult:

Exercise #3

What do you do better than family members, friends, classmates, co-workers, playmates?

Exercise #4

If you were at a party with every important person in your life (friends, family, teachers, bosses, lovers, spouse), what would these people say about your talents, qualities, and skills?

Exercise #5

Think of your special qualities, skills, and talents. What would the world miss if you didn't exist?

After you've completed the above exercises, make a master list of your top ten qualities, skills, and talents. This master list will be-

come your blueprint for designing and creating a more fulfilling, meaningful career and life.

Discovering What Motivates You

Once you've identified what you naturally do well, the next step is to understand what motivates you—what activities interest you, what excites you, and what you enjoy doing. These are not always the same as your natural talents and abilities. I have a good friend who is a talented writer. He enjoys writing letters to family and friends but can't stand the thought of having to write professionally. Another friend loves downhill ski racing more than anything in life, but she doesn't have the talent necessary to win.

WHAT YOU LIKE TO DO

What Makes You Enthusiastic and Excites You

What You Enjoy Doing

What Interests You

Your Motivation

Exercise #6

List your favorite activities.

Favorite Activities

Grade School:

High School:

College:

Young Adult:

Adult:

Exercise #7

If you had to live a year in a spaceship, what activities would you miss the most?

Exercise #8

What do you love to do on your job?

Exercise #9

List the five most rewarding job assignments you've had. Next, list the five most rewarding things that you've done in your life.

Exercise #10

What do you love to do in your spare time? What are your hobbies?

Exercise #11

Complete this sentence: "I feel best when I'm . . ."

After you've completed the above exercises, add the top ten things that motivate you to your master list.

Identifying Your Greatest Strengths and Power

Finding the matches among your talents, skills, qualities, and what you like to do reveals your greatest strengths and power.

Using your strengths lets you live life to the fullest. You realize all of your potential and make the greatest possible contribution. Even when a talent doesn't match what you love to do, a skill and quality might be a good match. My friend who loved downhill racing wasn't talented enough to win races, but she had wonderful teaching skills and became a great ski instructor.

What You Do Well + What You Like To Do = Strengths and Power

Exercise #12

Write down what you do well in the circle on the left and what you like to do in the circle on the right. List items that overlap in the center. These are your strengths.

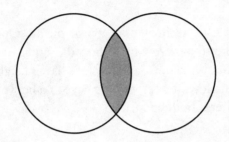

Exercise #13

List the accomplishments of which you are most proud.

Accomplishments

Grade School:

High School:

College:

Young Adult:

Adult:

What talents, skills and qualities did you utilize and how were you motivated?

Exercise #14

Think about your daydreams when you were a child, a teenager, a young adult, and an adult. What did you want to do, have, be? Don't analyze them; just write them down. After you've written them down, star the daydreams that utilize both what you do well and what you like to do.

Exercise #15

Imagine that you have reached your full potential. You are a success and people seek your advice. What do you look like? What is your day like? Where do you live? With whom do you spend your time? Write it down.

Exercise #16

Imagine that you are invited to appear on the Oprah Winfrey show. She introduces you by telling the audience what your friends, parents, loved ones, and teachers have said about you. All the people who love and respect you have told her your strengths. Write down her introduction.

Exercise #17

If you discovered that you had won the lottery and didn't need the money, how would you use your skills, qualities, and talents to help humanity?

Exercise #18

If you discovered that you had only five years to live, what would you do differently?

Exercise #19

If you could do anything that you wanted, what would you do? Why?

After you've completed the above exercises, add these strengths and daydreams to your master list.

DAY 2 ACTIVITIES AND EXERCISES

Activities

- Take an early-morning walk and watch the sunrise. Be thankful for the new day and new life that you are creating.

- Find a quiet, peaceful place, preferably outdoors, that nourishes your soul and complete Exercise #1, "Recurring Inner Messages." *Suggested time: 1–2 hours*
- Meditate 20 to 30 minutes.
- Read "Identifying the Right Environment," and complete Exercise #2. *Suggested time: 1–1½ hours*
- Take a midday break. Find a quiet place outdoors and practice a breathing exercise.
- Read "Identifying Your Values and Why Your Goals Need to Align With Them," and complete Exercise #3. *Suggested time: 1 hour*
- Exercise. Repeat your affirmations while exercising.
- Complete Exercise #4, "The Past, the Present, and the Future." *Suggested time: 1–1½ hours*
- Before or after dinner, take a Beauty break.
- Take an evening shower or bath. Wash away anything that might keep you from achieving your goals. Express gratitude for all the wonderful things that are happening in your life and for continued guidance and direction.
- Listen to relaxing music or a meditation tape before going to sleep.

Exercises

Exercise #1: Recurring Inner Messages

Review your journal and look at all the inner messages that you've recorded and highlighted during this program. On the left side of a piece of paper, make a list of all recurring messages. In the middle of the page, try to interpret these messages. On the far right, write down what action you should be taking.

RECURRING INNER MESSAGES	WHAT DOES THIS MEAN?	WHAT ACTION SHOULD I BE TAKING?

Next, take a clean piece of paper and draw a circle in the center of the page. On the outside of the circle, write down common messages, symbols, and insights. In the middle of the circle, write down what these messages suggest and what they have in common. If you are not clear, you can meditate, take a walk, or ask a question. If you're still unclear, set this exercise aside for a while. Ask your mind to help you interpret these messages and show you how to utilize your greatest strengths and talents.

Identifying the Right Environment

To find out how important your environment is, look at the plant and animal kingdoms. I learned some big lessons in this area the first year I started gardening. I had purchased a variety of my favorite flowers and proceeded to plant them in my backyard. I didn't research whether they needed full sun, partial sun, or partial shade. I didn't know what kinds of soil and water they needed. I just planted the flowers and waited for them to grow. After three weeks only half of my flowers survived. The rest had shriveled up, and despite my best efforts to revive them, they slowly died.

I learned about the impact of environment on plants the hard way. I might have known better because I, too, have thrived or shriveled up in various environments. In college I attended two different schools in two different parts of the country. Their credentials were quite similar, but the environments were entirely different. I was barely able to survive in one school, but in the other I thrived. I loved everything about it — the people, the community, the professors, and the classes. I have also discovered I blossom in certain cities and corporate environments, while in others I struggle just to keep going.

Environment is more than our physical surroundings; it also includes the people we're around. In a job it includes whether we work as part of a team, as individuals, as the boss, as a subordinate, in a large company, in a medium-sized company, in a small company, or as an independent. Being in the right environment can help us do our best work and allow us to thrive, prosper, and feel fulfilled. Being in the wrong environment can hinder us and hold us back.

Exercise #2: *The Right Environment for You*

Take some time to think about the environment in which you would like to live and work. Consider different areas of the country and take into account the weather.

Think about whether you'd like to live and work in a city, what surroundings you enjoy, and whether you like to spend time indoors or outside. Think about the people in your life. What are they like? Consider whether you want to work for yourself or in a company, how large the company would be, and what the work surroundings would look like. Are they beautifully furnished? Do you see individual offices, cubicles, a factory line, or an outdoor environment? In what field are you working: high technology, government, sports, fashion, television, nutrition, science, or some other area? What does your home environment look like?

After taking some time to think, write a description of your ideal environment. Describe in detail what it looks like, where it is, and the type of people who are around you. The more detailed you are, the easier it will be to manifest what you desire.

Identifying Your Values and Why Your Goals Need to Align with Them

Your values define what you believe is important in life. Your goals should be in harmony with your values. Some values are:

Security	Intelligence	Recognition
Independence	Fun	Friends
Status	Adventure	Helping others
Freedom	Happy workplace	Personal recognition
Family	Honesty	Love
Power	Teamwork	Support
High pay	Lots of time off	Structure

Some people make the mistake of choosing goals that are in conflict with their values. Fred values personal recognition and loves praise. He works in a high-tech firm that values teamwork and gives very little personal recognition. The team gets praise, but no individual on the team gets singled out for a job well done. As long as he places a high value on personal recognition, he will have a hard time being happy in this environment.

Claudia values security but dreams of starting her own small business in a field that is very risky. It's possible that her need for security could sabotage her success in this field.

Janet works part-time as a consultant. She loves her work but also values her family, friends, and free time. She is in the process of securing a large contract with an aerospace company. If she gets the contract, she will have to work 12-hour days and weekends. Having to work long hours will conflict with her value of spending time with family and friends.

Another friend of mine values beauty and has struggled with her job in a company that is a sea of bland gray cubicles.

Make sure that whatever goals you choose align with your values. If they don't, you could sabotage your success and satisfaction.

Exercise #3: Your Values

Take some time to be quiet and still and to think about what you value. When you're ready, list your top ten values and why they are important to you. If you have a hard time thinking about what you value, consider what you *don't* value. Identifying what you don't value can also help define what is important to you.

Exercise #4: The Past, the Present, and the Future

You can often learn something about the future by looking at the present and the past. If you are unhappy in your current situation or have been unhappy with past situations, use this exercise to examine why.

Draw four columns on a piece of paper. On the far left side, list as quickly as possible the reasons that you're unhappy. Think of what skills, qualities, and talents aren't being used, what needs are not being met, what values might be in conflict with your goals, and whether or not you are in the right environment.

In the next column, write down why this makes you unhappy. Again, write your answers down as quickly as possible. In the third column, list the things that make you happy in your current situation. What skills, qualities, and talents do you enjoy using? What things do you love doing? Finally, in the far right column, list what you would change to make it better. What would you change, and what would you leave the same?

WHY UNHAPPY?	ANALYZE WHY	WHAT MAKES ME HAPPY?	WHAT SHOULD I CHANGE?

Go back and star all the items that are most important to you. Add these to your master list. These are the key ingredients you need to be happy, fulfilled, and content.

DAY 3 ACTIVITIES AND EXERCISES

Activities

Today you'll be doing several brainstorming exercises. You'll be using Blue Sky exercises to free yourself of limiting thoughts and open up the powers of your mind to think clearly and creatively. Blue skies allow for infinite possibilities. You can reach to the heavens or reach for your star. Before you start, make sure you've cleared away all possible cloud cover. Gray skies can cast a shadow on future possibilities. It's best to do these exercises when your mind is open and free. Be like a child—open, inquisitive, playful, and curious.

To get in the right frame of mind, you might want to do some of the things that you did as a child. Young children are very imaginative and creative. Think of a time before parents, teachers, and peers stifled your creativity. Let your mind be childlike, full of wonder, full of creativity, full of possibilities. Let your imagination have no limits. Think back to a time when you giggled and were carefree, a time when you looked up at the sky and watched the clouds float by.

- Take an early-morning shower. Imagine all limiting thoughts being washed away. As you shower, think of ten ways you could restructure your life and career to leverage your greatest strengths. Towel-dry quickly and write them down. Don't spend a lot of time thinking; just write.
- Go for a long walk or hike after breakfast. Spend some time thinking about the new life you want to create. Ask yourself if there is anything better for you than you imagined. Gaze at the sky and watch the clouds go by if it helps your mind be expansive.
- Complete Exercise #1, "The Big Picture: Long-Term Goals." *Suggested time: 1 hour*
- Read "How to Set Clear, Specific Goals to Get What You Want," and "Tips for Setting Goals."
- Find a quiet, peaceful place and complete Exercise #2, "Goals Not Working." *Suggested time: 1–1½ hours*
- Take a time-out! Take a break from the activities and exercises and enjoy the afternoon. Go exploring, take a nap, read an inspirational book. Have your notebook handy.
- Go for a walk at twilight. Breathe slowly and deeply and observe the energy around you. Think about your long-term goals. Think about possibilities and what you'd like to accomplish in the next six months.
- Listen to relaxing music or a meditation tape before you go to sleep.

Exercises

Exercise #1: *The Big Picture: Long-Term Goals*

Think of your entire life stretched before you. Write down as quickly as possible what you would like to be, do, and have in this lifetime in these areas:

Career	Educational	Travel/Adventures
Spiritual	Financial	Pleasure
Health and fitness	Contribution	Friends
Family	Residence	

Next, imagine that you're ninety-eight years old. Looking back on your life, is there anything that you regret not being, doing, or having? What would you like to be remembered for? Again, write down your responses as quickly as possible.

This is a list of your long-term goals. Some of them will change from time to time. Try to review your long-term goals annually and make any needed revisions. Add these goals to your master list. Make sure that they are consistent with your values, that they allow you to utilize your strengths and to live and work in your ideal environment.

How to Set Clear, Specific Goals to Get What You Want

The best way to get what you want is to set specific goals and direct your thinking and actions toward achieving those goals. If you want a new career, more money, a better relationship, a new car, a slim and fit body, a trip around the world, or to redecorate your home, set a goal. When you set a clear, specific goal, you can accomplish anything you want.

A goal is like a compass. It helps you to stay headed in the right direction, navigate your way through uncharted waters, keep on course, and reach your destination. Goals help you to prioritize your day-to-day activities and be more efficient and focused so that you can free up more time and energy.

I began setting goals in junior high school. At the time my goals were pretty vague. I wanted to improve my faith, think positively all the time, smile a lot, pick a career, form an environmental club, and have a more harmonious family life. For years I would add or subtract a goal every New Year's Day. I was setting goals just to set goals. I didn't necessarily believe that any of them would come true. They weren't measurable, and I had no real desire to make them come true. Eventually a friend and I did organize an environmental club, and in due time I did select a career—but if I'd been more clear about what I wanted, I could have accomplished more.

On the other hand, I would make a wish on my birthday every year and it always came true. Why did my wishes come true and not my goals? For one thing, my wishes were very succinct and clear. I had to make a wish quickly before blowing out the candles on my cake. Also, I'd wish for something that I really wanted. I'd close my eyes and imagine it for a moment and then I would clearly ask for my wish to come true. My goals were often just words—words I didn't really believe in. I wanted to be better and brighter and happier, but I wasn't specific about why or how, and I didn't really imagine that my goals would come true. I did believe that my wishes would come true.

Motivational experts say that only about 10 percent of all people set goals, and I can understand why. Why bother if it's just an exercise in writing words down on paper? What do those words mean? Can you imagine actually living these words? Of the 10 percent who write down their goals annually, only a small percentage ever accomplish them. For the most part, it's because they can't imagine actually achieving their goals. I know some people who write down the same goals year after year. They don't accomplish them, so they write them down again the next year. Obviously something is not working.

Successful people who routinely set and achieve goals all agree that goals need to be clear, specific, and measurable. They must be things you truly desire and things you believe you can have.

Tips for Setting Goals

1. *Be as clear and specific as possible.* No generalizing, as I did in junior high. If you want to improve your faith, be clear and specific about why and how. What's the benefit? Vague goals produce vague results. If you want to make more money, be very specific about how much money you want to make, why you want to make it, how it will benefit you, and what you intend to do with it.

Old goal:	To make more money
New goal:	To make $100,000 annually
What's the benefit?	To continue living in the style to which my family has grown accustomed; to save for retirement; to take my family to Hawaii at Christmas; to buy a new car; to give 10% to charity
Why do I need $100,000?	Net income (after taxes) is $70,000; monthly expenses are $4,000, or $48,000 annually; Christmas gifts are $2,000; vacation to Hawaii is $3,000; charitable donations are $7,000; retirement and savings are $7,000; new car payments are $3,000

2. *Determine what you will do to get your goal, and commit to doing it.* This includes time, energy, and money commitments. Many people want things but are unwilling to pay the price. What is the price and are you willing to pay it?

What am I willing to do to make $100,000? I am willing to change jobs if necessary, to make ten cold calls a week, to join three new organizations to meet potential clients and network, and to take on three new projects at work.

3. *Set a date by which you will accomplish the goal.* Make sure that your date is realistic, and determine how you will know when you've attained your goal.

Date: July 15, 20—
Measurement: Bank statement, pay stub

4. *Make sure that you truly desire this goal.* It's easier to accomplish a goal when you have a strong desire to do so. A good friend of mine was financially strapped when she learned about an opportunity to go to Africa. It was something that she'd always wanted to do—a chance of a lifetime. She needed to raise $5,000. It was the easiest $5,000 she ever made. The desire was there, so the money flowed easily.

5. *Work on only seven to ten goals at a time.* After you've determined your long-term goals, select seven to ten goals from that list that you want to work on in the next six months.

6. *Create a visualization, affirmation, and action plan* on paper to make your goals come true, and begin taking action immediately!

Exercise #2: Goals Not Working

If you've written goals that have never been realized, try doing this exercise. Ask yourself these questions: What is the goal? Why do you want this goal? Why haven't you achieved it? Why haven't you done the things you needed to do to achieve it? What do you need to work on to achieve this goal? Will you work on this item?

Here's an example of how this exercise might work:

What is the goal?	To get promoted
Why do you want this goal?	More money, status, prestige
Why haven't you achieved it?	Haven't promoted self, missed deadlines, disorganized, haven't kept boss informed
Why haven't you done the things you needed to do to achieve it?	Low self-esteem, poor organizational and time-management skills
What do you need to work on to achieve this goal?	Improve self-esteem, take time-management classes, keep boss informed
Are you committed to working on this?	Yes

This exercise will help you discover the real reason you haven't reached your goal. If there's a goal that you've been trying to achieve year after year, ask yourself if you really want it and whether or not you're willing to do whatever it takes to achieve this goal.

DAY 4 ACTIVITIES AND EXERCISES

Activities

- Meditate.
- Complete Exercise #1, "Short-Term Goals." *Suggested time: 2–3½ hours*
- Exercise.
- Read "The Importance of Visualizations and Affirmations" and complete Exercise #2. *Suggested time: 1–1½ hours*
- Take a midday break.
- Complete Exercise #3, "Affirmations." *Suggested time: 1–1½ hours*
- Go for a walk at twilight. Think about what steps you need to take to accomplish your goals. Repeat each of your new affirmations ten times.

- Prepare for an evening bath or shower. Light candles. Put on soft, soothing music. Use a muscle relaxation exercise and relax all the muscles in your body. Close your eyes and visualize achieving your goals.
- Listen to relaxing music or a meditation tape before you go to sleep.

Exercises

Exercise #1: Short-Term Goals

To walk a mile, you must begin with the first step. To walk 10 miles, you must first learn to walk a mile. The best way to accomplish long-term goals is to break them down into achievable short-term goals.

When I decided to run a marathon, I had to set weekly and monthly running goals that were easy to accomplish and got me in the proper shape to run 26 miles. There was no way that I could decide to run a marathon and then just go out and do it. I would have injured or killed myself and never achieved my goal.

Take a look at your long-term goals. Which excite you most? Star the ones that you would most like to work on in the next six months, and break them down into doable, achievable goals. Select seven to ten short-term goals. Then write clear, concise statements of the goal, the benefit, your commitment, when you plan to achieve the short-term goal, how you'll measure it, and why you desire this goal.

The Importance of Visualizations and Affirmations

After writing clear, concise, short-term goal statements, think of them as if they were already reality.

Remember, your thoughts create your reality. Napoleon Hill, author of *Think and Grow Rich*, tells us that whatever the mind can conceive and believe, it can achieve. We need to imagine our success in advance of getting it. Visualizations and affirmations are powerful tools for evoking the feeling of already having our goals and for directing our energy toward attracting to us what we want. When we mix our thoughts with intense feelings, we generate energy that is like a laser beam and draws our dreams into physical reality.

To visualize your goal, focus on a thought or picture of the goal in your mind. See yourself as already having the goal. What does it look like? How do you feel? Imagine it vividly and intensely, using all your senses. Next, write down what you see and feel. Here are two visualizations that were created after writing goal statements.

1. *I am a communications consultant. I counsel with clients, pinpoint their communications needs, and pull together and manage teams to complete projects. I do a great job and work efficiently so that I have enough time off to enjoy my after-work lifestyle. My job provides great pay and benefits and allows me to telecommute from home.*

I work in a beautiful office. I have an oil painting above my desk and fresh flowers on the credenza behind me. I work for a small company that is well respected. My co-workers are intelligent, fun-loving, spontaneous, caring, kind, and ethical. I have a great rapport with my co-workers and clients.

My work offers opportunities for travel, learning, variety, contact with interesting people, and independence. I give thanks for my wonderful job.

2. *I wake up to sunlight streaming into the room. It's summertime. I get out of bed and walk down the hall to my study. French doors open out into the courtyard, and I have a skylight over my desk. I see a big tree outside and birds are singing. My study is light and airy. I have lots of bookshelves and a fireplace. It's very comfortable. I sink into a comfy chair and meditate. At 6:30 A.M., I take my two dogs for a walk. We live in the country, and I walk past my*

*garden to a beautiful trail in the woods. I come back and shower in
my French-tiled bathroom. I select clothes from my walk-in closet
and have breakfast with my husband on the patio. We have freshly
squeezed orange juice and read* The New York Times. *There are
fresh flowers on the table. The living and dining room have hardwood floors and lots of throw rugs. There is pine furniture in the
gourmet kitchen. It's clean and spacious.*

*I work in a nearby city in an old Victorian house. I greet my as-
sistant, who manages the office. She's a wonderful, energetic person,
very positive and filled with love.*

If you have difficulty creating a mental image, find pictures
in magazines to help you visualize your goals. A good friend of mine
wanted a red convertible, so she cut out a picture of her face and
pasted it into an advertisement for a red convertible. She would look
at the picture and could easily see herself in the new red car. She
could even feel the wind in her hair. Within six months she was the
proud owner of a red Toyota Celica convertible!

Exercise #2: *Visualization Meditation*

Find a spot that's peaceful and quiet. Make sure that you will not
be disturbed for at least an hour. Find a comfortable sitting position and have your notebook and pen nearby. Remember to keep
your spine straight to allow good energy flow.

1. Close your eyes and begin breathing slowly and calmly. Take
   10 to 20 slow, deep breaths. Be aware of your breath moving
   in and out. As you inhale, say, "I receive." As you exhale, say,
   "I let go." Let go of any tension in your body. Exhale all the
   tension until you begin to feel calm and peaceful.
2. Relax your body. Using the muscle relaxation technique,
   travel through your body, relaxing each area. You can also
   imagine a flame of white light going through your body, removing all impurities and tensions. Feel yourself growing
   serene and calm.

3. Focus on your goal. Imagine yourself having the goal. Picture it as clearly as possible. What do you see? Utilize all of your senses. Can you see it in color? Imagine the feelings you will have. If any negative thoughts surface, imagine sweeping them away with a broom.
4. When you feel calm and relaxed and are ready open your eyes, take a few moments to slowly reorient yourself. Take some deep breaths and stretch.
5. Write down your visualization. Be as detailed as possible.

Exercise #3: Affirmations

Next, write down affirmations for all your goals. Include affirmations to release blockages if you have any. These will help you direct your energy toward creating what you want. Say these affirmations aloud at least ten times every day and express gratitude for what you have achieved. Bob created the following affirmations:

I am a success.
I am a highly paid executive and respected by customers, co-workers, and employees.
I have plenty of free time to work on my hobbies.
I am healthy and vibrant.
I have a wonderful, supportive relationship with my wife.

DAY 5 ACTIVITIES AND EXERCISES

Activities

- Get up early and watch the sunrise. Think about your new goals and how you are going to achieve them. Say your affirmations ten times.
- Meditate.
- Read "Action!" and complete Exercise #1. *Suggested time: 3–4 hours*

- *Enjoy a Clarity Quest Celebration!*
  Find a beautiful, sacred place. Bring along your journal,
  your new blueprint for the future.
  Soak in the beauty. Close your eyes and breathe slowly
  and deeply 20 times. Holding your new blueprint in your
  hand, give thanks for the creation of your new future. Bless
  your goals. Know that they are for your highest good, and
  ask that they be for the highest good of all concerned. See
  yourself living your goals and enjoying your new life. See
  your greatness. Offer your full commitment to your new
  life and vow to make it happen.
- Reward yourself for completing all the activities and exercises. Have a glass of champagne or sparkling cider. Light
  a candle. Reflect on all the wonderful things that you've
  learned these last eight weeks. Express gratitude for the
  new meaning and direction in your life. Make a wish and
  blow out the candle.
- Ask yourself what one action you can take today to help you
  achieve your goals, and DO IT!

Exercises

Action!

Now it's time to put your plan on paper and to outline all the steps
you will take to achieve your goal. This becomes your personal
game plan and details everything that you need to *act on* to make
your goal a reality. Action plans also help you to monitor your
progress so you keep moving forward, or let you know when cor-
rective action is necessary.

Successful action plans include three elements:

1. What needs to be done
2. How it will be done
3. When it will be done

Here's what an action plan might look like for the goal "Explore PR opportunities in five to ten industry segments."

What:	_By when:_
Research and identify all industries best suited to my values, strengths, and ideal environment	

How:

1. Visit library research desk; ask how to investigate various industries	_Sept. 5_
2. Research all material available, including Fortune 500 annual list	_Sept. 5–9_
3. Research professional and business organizations, directories, and registries	_Sept. 10_

What:

Select top 5–10 industries that I'm interested in

What:

Contact everyone I know in these industries

How:

1. Create contact list; ask friends for names of people they know	_Sept. 15_
2. Call these people and set up informational interviews	_Sept. 16–30_
3. Ask for referrals, including PR people in these industries	_Sept. 16–30_

What:

Identify companies in these industries

How:

1. Create list of companies	*Oct. 1*
2. Call these companies directly for annual reports and brochures	*Oct. 2–5*
3. Review annual reports, brochures, notes	*Oct. 15–31*
4. Create list of people I know/referrals in these companies	*Oct. 15*

What:

Identify PR job opportunities in these companies

How:

1. Call list of referrals, above, set up informational interviews, and ask for more referrals	*Nov. 1–5*
2. Call PR and business communication associations and headhunters regarding job opportunities in these companies	*Oct. 15–31*
3. Review want ads, check out who's hiring	*Nov. 1–5*

What:

Write down industries, companies, and PR opportunities.

You're now ready for your next goal, which is to begin job hunting. You might have discovered a wonderful job opportunity during one of the informational interviews. If it's a perfect fit, go for it!

At the beginning of each day, ask yourself which activities will help you realize your goal. Make those activities your priority, and do them! Reward yourself often for what you accomplish. Review your visualizations daily and your action plan once a week. You'll have a sense of satisfaction when you cross off items you've accomplished, and you'll know just what to do the next week to stay on track.

Exercise #1: Action Plan

Look over your goal statements, visualizations, and affirmations. For each goal, write down everything you can imagine doing to achieve what you want. These are your action items. Next, prioritize them and say when you'll accomplish each one. Add your action plan to your blueprint.

Chapter 10

Clarity Quest Pioneers

▓ Pioneers are courageous people who venture ahead to explore new territories, blaze new trails, and prepare the way for others to follow. We can learn a tremendous amount from them. Their experiences give us insight into what lies ahead, which helps us prepare for our own journey.

I'm grateful to all the Clarity Quest Pioneers—people from a variety of professions and different parts of the country who participated in this program to help make it more meaningful and accessible. They gave freely of their time not only because they wanted to improve their own lives, but also because they wanted to help others.

These pioneer stories show how you can take control of your life. You can feel healthier and better about yourself, tap into the powers of the subconscious mind, break free of analysis paralysis, get clear about what you want, and create your best possible life and livelihood.

I hope their stories inspire you and encourage you to continue on your journey toward a more satisfying, fulfilling life.

SARAH'S STORY
Clear Focus, New Opportunities

Sarah, a human resources manager for a marketing consulting company, had been worried about losing her job for two years. The company's profits were down, and the upper-level management team had tossed around several restructuring plans. She knew all about them. Her boss had been involved in these meetings and had talked candidly to her staff. Sarah's fears left her paralyzed and unable to explore other job opportunities in her company or elsewhere.

When Sarah started the Clarity Quest program, she was filled with fear and hadn't been sleeping well. She had two small children and was finding it difficult to juggle her own needs with those of her family. She wasn't sure that she could complete the eight-week program, but after the first few weeks she was sleeping better and feeling more relaxed. She decided to go the distance and committed to finishing her Clarity Quest. She made a positive statement to herself and others that she was willing to take control of her own life and career.

The minute she decided to take control, some wonderful things started to happen. Out of the blue, an old classmate called and wanted to get together for lunch. Her classmate was involved in a start-up software development company and wanted to know if Sarah was interested in joining the team. Sarah was flattered but not sure if she was ready to make the move.

She continued working through her Clarity Quest and scheduled her week-long getaway. During that time she brainstormed several different career possibilities, which helped her clarify what she wanted to do and the direction she wanted to take. Her friend's job offer was tempting, but during the getaway Sarah discovered that she valued a regular paycheck and liked working regular eight-hour days. The new job possibility wouldn't be a good match for her. She saw that she enjoyed working in human resources but wanted something more stable.

When Sarah returned from her getaway, she called her class-mate to talk about her decision. They discussed the direction Sarah wanted to take, and her friend graciously gave her the name of someone to call in a large, stable company. Sarah made the call and, to her delight, discovered that the company was interviewing for a human resources position. She applied and got the job.

Sarah learned that when you make a commitment to take action, your fears begin to dissolve. When you open your mind to new possibilities, exciting things start to happen.

ROBERT'S STORY
Breaking Away

Robert, a divorce attorney in his late forties, wanted out. He was tired of dealing with bickering and unhappy clients and was weary of courtroom politics. He had been dreaming about other careers for years and even had a file drawer full of newspaper clippings, magazine articles, and lists of the various careers he'd explored. Several sounded interesting: managing a bed and breakfast inn on the coast, becoming a winemaker, working for a nonprofit environmental organization, teaching and writing. His file kept growing, and so did his discontent. Robert was on the verge of making a breakthrough but suffered from analysis paralysis.

His wife finally put her foot down. She told him that it was time to stop talking and start taking action. She recommended the Clarity Quest program, and he responded enthusiastically. He felt that if he had a little more data to analyze, he would be able to make a well-informed decision about what to do with the rest of his life.

About midway through the Clarity Quest program, Robert started taking long walks in the evening along a trail through the woods near his home. Walking helped him unwind from the pressures of the day and get quiet enough to listen to his inner thoughts and feelings. He had many new insights about the careers he was contemplating. Some made him feel tense and anxious, and gave him a heavy feeling in his gut. Thinking about others made him feel joyful and excited.

During his week-long retreat, Robert did a lot of walking and listening. He used this inner guidance to gather the courage to take the first concrete steps toward a new career. He selected three areas to explore: teaching, environmental lobbying, and managing a bed and breakfast inn. He'd already collected a lot of data but felt that he lacked real-life experience in these areas.

He gave himself a time limit. In six months he would make a final decision. He knew a professor at the local university and offered to be a teaching assistant without payment. He committed to spending one night a week with the professor, and all he asked in return was the opportunity to observe and learn. Next, he signed up to work on a committee at the local environmental group so that he would meet members and learn firsthand some of the challenges that they faced. The last item in his action plan was to spend four weekends at popular bed and breakfast inns along the coast. He scheduled appointments to talk to the owners and learn about the challenges and opportunities.

Robert had finally broken free of analysis paralysis. He'd used his inner guidance to determine what he wanted, and then followed up his insights with action.

ERIC'S AND LAURA'S STORIES
Starting Over

Eric had been living with his girlfriend Sally for five years. They had similar interests and enjoyed many of the same activities. It was a comfortable relationship, but Sally sensed that it wasn't going anywhere. She wanted to get married, buy a home, and start a family. Eric wasn't ready to commit. He wasn't sure that he wanted Sally to be his life partner. After an amicable discussion, they decided to break up. Eric helped Sally find a new apartment and helped her move in.

Six months later Eric received a letter from Sally. It was a classic "Dear John" letter. She wrote that she'd found someone new and was moving to Seattle to finish her MBA. Eric was devastated. His first impulse was to catch the next plane to Seattle and propose. He reread the letter and realized that the most troubling part was not that he was losing her but that she had moved on and he hadn't. She was starting a new life, and he felt trapped in a dead-end job and didn't have anyone in his life.

Clarity Quest helped Eric assess what he really wanted. He felt better about his decision not to marry Sally and mapped out a new future for himself. He became involved in Habitat for Humanity because he wanted to help others and see the results of his efforts. He loves the work and is very good at it. He's now dating a woman that he met through a volunteer at work. And he's nuts about her.

Laura's husband left her, and her world was turned upside down. She'd thought she had the "perfect" marriage, only to discover that her husband had been seeing another woman for years. Five months after their breakup, he wanted to come back. She was cautious. She hated living alone and was worried about money. Still, she liked the person she was becoming outside the marriage.

Laura used Clarity Quest to help her define what she really wanted and valued. She spent a lot of time meditating, reflecting, and daydreaming. She started eating better and going on long walks with a friend. She joined a women's group and started applying effective time-management techniques to help her stop feeling overwhelmed. She discovered a new inner strength that helped her follow through with her decision. She decided to divorce her husband, heal the past, and start over.

JANE'S STORY
Overcoming Feelings of Failure
and Low Self-Worth

Ten years ago Jane was a high-powered saleswoman for an electronics company. She quit her job shortly after being passed up for a promotion. She was a great salesperson, but deep inside she didn't believe in the products that she was selling and didn't feel appreciated for her efforts.

She went to work for a friend who owned a small advertising and marketing company. Two years later she quit. She'd done a tremendous job helping to grow the company but didn't feel recognized or valued for her contributions and still wasn't sure that she was on the right career path. Again, she didn't really believe in the products she'd helped promote.

Four companies later, she realized that she was very good at helping others to succeed in their chosen fields but continued to feel like an outsider. She realized that she'd never felt satisfied or fulfilled in any job. She wanted to feel passionate about what she did and about the company for which she worked. And she wanted to be recognized and valued for her contributions.

Before she started the Clarity Quest program, Jane had taken a class to discover her life's purpose and passion. No great insights had come to her. No bells had rung. No whistles had gone off. She wasn't clear about what she wanted to do, and she was extremely frustrated that in all of her career meanderings, she hadn't come across the perfect job.

When Jane worked on the Forgiveness and Acceptance exercises, she made an interesting discovery. She was holding herself back. She saw herself as a failure because she'd changed careers so frequently and hadn't found the job of her dreams. Since she had "failed" so many times, she had started to feel that somehow she didn't deserve to be happy in her work. Jane had a habit of berating herself and had labeled herself a failure. Her self talk was filled with words like "loser," "lacking direction and purpose," and "wishy-washy." She realized that she couldn't become a success until she stopped thinking of herself as a failure and started believing that she was a worthy and deserving person.

To help move beyond these feelings of failure, Jane made a list of all the valuable skills and lessons she'd learned over the past ten years. She also listed her accomplishments and successes. It was quite a long list. She then made a list of all the people, emotions, and beliefs that were holding her back—and she held a beautiful ceremony to release them.

Throughout the program Jane realized that she had to send her subconscious mind messages that she was a worthy and deserving person. She took time to nurture herself and affirm her value. She worked to change her self talk, affirming frequently that she'd done the best she knew how to do at the time, that all the lessons and skills she'd acquired were valuable, and that she had a unique and special contribution to make.

During the retreat she inventoried all her talents and skills and probed to find her true motivations. She realized that she enjoyed helping others but needed more control over her own job responsibilities. In her previous jobs she had always worked as part of a team. That had made it hard to get the praise and acknowledgment that she sought as an individual.

When Jane reviewed her skills, successes, and lessons learned, then coupled them with her innate selling abilities, she saw that she had some powerful tools that she could use to launch her own company. She spent two days during the retreat mapping out a business plan for herself and wrote down a beautiful visualization clearly detailing her new life. She described what she would be doing, what her office would look like, what she would be wearing, and how it would feel to be successful and deserving.

Jane started her own company, which helps small businesses and individuals design and implement their own marketing and sales plans. She is excited about running her own enterprise and about helping others. Finally she is passionate about her work and knows that she can make a valuable contribution.

ED'S STORY
Same Job, New Organization, New Life

Ed lost his job suddenly after working for the same company for twenty-five years. He was looking for a new job and decided to go through the Clarity Quest program because he knew that he should be at his best while he was in the process of searching for a new position. He had been out of work for only a week, but he could already see how easy it was to get off track. He found himself struggling constantly with low self-esteem, loss of identity, disbelief, anger, and fear.

Ed was very frightened when he first started Clarity Quest. He wasn't ready for retirement but wasn't sure that he had any valuable or transferable skills. He'd been in middle management for many years, he was twenty pounds overweight, he smoked, and he didn't exercise.

Ed welcomed the daily activities of the Clarity Quest program. They gave him something to do while he pursued the classifieds every day and talked to headhunters. He really didn't think that he would be changing his life much; he just wanted to get on with it.

Much to his surprise, Clarity Quest did change his life—for the better. He started practicing the breathing exercises and meditation, eating healthy foods, and going on long walks in the evening. He had more energy and started feeling better about himself. Ed lost ten pounds in the first month and felt like he'd also lost ten years. He started taking nature hikes and looking forward to a new outdoor adventure every weekend. Ed felt happier and healthier than he had felt in a long time. He organized his home and office and eliminated clutter. He felt more vibrant and relaxed, both physically and emotionally, than he ever had.

Ed interviewed for the same position in another company and was their first choice. He has rerouted his life in positive directions and is looking forward to working another twenty-five years for his new company.

MARIANNE'S AND JACK'S STORIES
Finding the Balance

Marianne was a successful real estate agent who longed to use her degree in art history, but lived in a small community that didn't even have an art museum. She often felt frustrated, but her family didn't want to move to a large city where there would be lots of museums and galleries.

During her retreat Marianne revisited her greatest talents, skills, and what she liked doing. She was a great communicator and loved talking about great works of art. She also loved painting and teaching. She saw a way to use these strengths while continuing to make a living in real estate. Marianne is planning to teach art history classes in a local junior college one night a week and to paint with passion on the weekends.

Jack, a talented actor, had loved performing in plays in high school and college. He loved everything about the theater and was seriously considering quitting his job to pursue a full-time career in acting. During his Clarity Quest he found that he didn't want to give up his job. He valued the money and security too much and didn't want to make any sacrifices.

He decided instead to get involved in a local theater group. Jack is currently starring in a lead role and has also begun working on a script. He's not sure where this will take him, but he's happier now because he's doing things he loves.

JILL'S STORY
Staying the Course

Jill, an award-winning television director, wasn't getting enough work to pay the rent. She was $20,000 in debt and decided it was time to explore some other career options. She also hoped that Clarity Quest would help her find a way to get out of debt.

During the program she worked to identify her natural talents, skills, and motivations. It did not surprise her to discover that she'd already found the perfect job. She loved being a director. Her work excited and motivated her and leveraged her greatest strengths. She also realized that she had a special talent for visualizing successful programs. For years she had practiced mentally walking through each stage of a production, seeing the crew and talent all performing at their best.

During the retreat, she got up early one morning to watch the sunrise. She reflected on her predicament. She was in the right career, loved what she was doing, and was very good at it. She wondered why she couldn't find enough work to meet her expenses. Jill put together a financial plan during the second week of the program and knew exactly how much money she needed to meet expenses. She knew the average amount she made for each show and the number of shows that she would have to direct each year in order to stay solvent. It wasn't a large number, and she certainly had the ability to do it.

She decided to formulate one good question and to ask it over and over until she had a clear answer and direction. She asked, "What do I need to do to attract wonderful projects that will gross $70,000 a year?"

She asked the question at sunrise and sunset each day. The answer came to her on the second day: She needed to spend as much time and energy visualizing *getting programs to direct* as she did visualizing the programs themselves. She spent the day thinking about the type of clients that she wanted to attract and mentally rehearsing meetings with them, telling them what she had to offer. She wrote down her visualization and brainstormed ways to meet these clients.

Jill worked on a plan to market herself. She outlined all the steps she needed to take in order to meet these clients: calling all her current clients and friends and asking for referrals, identifying groups and meetings to attend, and practicing her visualization daily.

Jill felt confident that she could begin to attract projects immediately. She knew what she wanted to do and was very clear about how to get it.

These Clarity Quest Pioneers broke new ground to find the life of their dreams, and you can too. Let their stories inspire you, and jump in!

Chapter 11

Beyond Clarity Quest: Your New Frontier

The embers were still warm and glowing softly. The fire that had blazed so brightly was fading. It was the last night I would spend in this high mountain place, and I was reluctant to go to bed. I watched the embers flicker and stirred the coals, trying to reignite the flame. I tried to remember its warmth and wondered if I would recall the magic of this place when I returned home. Would the new trails I'd discovered and the new things I'd learned still be real for me? I gazed at the embers for a good long while. Eventually a voice answered. I hardly recognized it as my own. "Store the memories in your heart and go there often. Everything you need to remember is stored deep within."

— JOURNAL ENTRY

Have you ever taken a wonderful, relaxing vacation and then, within a few days of your return, gotten so caught up in the daily grind that you almost forgot you ever went away? It's easy to get so caught up in our To Do's that we forget our purpose. We forget to remember where we've been and where we're headed.

During the last two months you've worked to renew your energy, build new habits, and design a more satisfying life. You should be feeling healthier, more vibrant, and more alive than ever before, and very enthusiastic about the life you want to create.

Three simple maintenance routines will help keep your energy and thinking focused after the Quest:

- Daily Conditioning
- Weekly Checkups
- Quarterly Tune-ups

These routines guide you through reviewing your goals and making sure you're headed in the right direction. Of course, you should continue to exercise, meditate, eat healthy, and build Silence and Solitude breaks and Nature and Beauty breaks into your schedule. Loving yourself and caring for your physical and emotional health should not end with your Clarity Quest.

DAILY CONDITIONING

Successful athletes, actors, world leaders, business leaders, writers, and teachers share a simple success formula: *They first believe that they can succeed, and then they spend the necessary time and energy preparing mentally for their success.*

Do you believe that you can accomplish your goals? Do you believe you can be successful? If so, you will probably accomplish everything you set out to achieve. If you're hesitant or lack confidence, you may need time to grow into the person you want to become.

I know a talented director who spends several days just sitting around a table with the actors before they begin rehearsals, talking about the script and characters. These discussions help the actors flesh out their characters and prompt any rewrites that may be necessary. Next, they block out their movements. By the time rehearsals begin, the actors have a clear understanding of the characters they're going to portray. They know how their characters look, feel, move, and respond. During rehearsals they polish their roles, slowly building confidence in their ability to bring those characters to life. By the time the curtain goes up, they're ready to give an excellent performance.

You can use these same techniques to prepare yourself for success. Management consultants frequently advise people who want to be promoted to act as if they have already been given the new job. They urge their clients to find out how a manager at the next level dresses, moves, and acts—and to start doing those same things. If you pay attention to the small details of dress, speech, and behavior, you send a message to yourself and others that you're ready to move up.

Four guidelines can help you condition yourself for success on a daily basis:

1. *Take a cleansing shower each morning.* Mentally wash away all negative emotions and thoughts that block energy and prevent you from reaching your goals.

2. *Spend time every morning visualizing your success.* Find role models who are already doing the things that you've dreamed of doing. Find out how they approach life and what they do on a daily basis. Incorporate these things into the visualization that you worked on during your Quest. Picturing success in your mind focuses your energy and helps you prioritize daily activities. The more time you spend thinking about the person you want to become, the greater the probability that you will become that person.

3. *Do something each day that will help you realize your goal.* Identifying one thing to do each day helps break down your goal into manageable steps. It's easy to do just one thing, and doing it builds confidence. You feel good about yourself, and at the same time you are moving closer to your goal.

4. Start a success file. Keep a log of everything you do that makes you feel successful. Think about the person you want to become, and note all the times you exhibit a characteristic of this new person. You can add things you've done in the past, such as being on a varsity team, winning a scholarship, or being promoted. Include praise from others. If you want to become a more loving and compassionate person, describe the times you've been compassionate. Refer to this file often, and let it serve as a constant reminder of the person you are growing into.

WEEKLY CHECKUPS

Reviewing your goals and progress on a weekly basis is an excellent way to stay focused and to make sure you keep heading in the right direction.

I once met with a very successful client in his tastefully decorated office. He was called away for a few moments, and I studied his environment carefully. The desk and credenza were made of beautiful koa wood. The desk was uncluttered, and books were stacked neatly on the credenza, which also showcased beautiful photographs of his family.

One picture looked different and stood out. It was a framed picture of his goals. They were right above his phone in a place where he would see them often. I had never seen such a prominent display of goals, and I asked him about it. He told me that he referred to them all the time. Often during disturbing phone calls, even during calls with his wife and children, he would glance at his goals and remember what was most important to him in life. It helped him to ignore the stuff that didn't matter and focus on what did matter.

Here are a few simple things you can do on a weekly basis to remind yourself of where you are going and help you map out how to get there.

1. Each week review your goals, tasks, and activities. This helps you be aware of what has been done, what is important to do, and what can wait. Make this review fun. Put on great music or go to a quiet park. You are creating a better life for yourself. Enjoy the process!

2. Make a list of _why_ you are committed to these goals and review it weekly. This will motivate you and remind you to stay focused—no matter what else is happening in your life.

3. Record and track your progress. Continue to record how you're feeling and what you've accomplished.

4. Map out activities for the upcoming week. Clearly define what needs to be done and prioritize these items. This will help you to focus your time and energy.

5. Express gratitude. Take time out each week to think about all the wonderful changes that are happening in your life. Write them down. This helps you keep perspective and opens up your heart to receive more good.

QUARTERLY TUNE-UPS

When you return home from your Quest, your life will no doubt be filled with a lot of business and distractions. You'll have phone calls to make, faxes to send, e-mails to review, friendships to tend to, partners to please, and bosses to appease.

Quarterly tune-ups—planned weekend getaways—help you get away from life's fast pace so that you can relax and renew your whole system. A weekend "away from it all" can work like magic, completely revitalizing your mind, body, and spirit. It's a wonderful antidote to a hectic schedule and lifestyle.

There are a number of ways to enjoy this kind of getaway. A good friend of mine spends a couple of days at a spiritual retreat and returns home feeling totally rejuvenated. During her two days away she meditates, takes long walks in the woods, and catches up on her sleep. Another friend spends his weekend "getaway" at home. He rents several videotapes and buys a book he's always wanted to read. He unplugs his phone and renews his energy by giving himself a few days of simply watching tapes and reading.

Family obligations or time limitations might make it difficult to take an entire weekend off. A one-day getaway can also be renewing and relaxing. A client of mine checks into a day spa to relax and unwind. She schedules a facial and massage and spends the rest of the day relaxing by the pool. She brings along an inspirational book, and by the end of the day she feels completely rested and recharged. Many people enjoy day outings to the beach, a quiet park, or an art museum.

The following stay-at-home revitalization weekend was designed to tune your body, mind, and spirit and leave you uplifted and energized.

REVITALIZATION WEEKEND

Preparation

- ✔ Buy groceries and supplies—foods that will cleanse your system, such as fruits, vegetables, brown rice, whole grain breads, and juices.
- ✔ Buy an inspirational book and rent inspirational videotapes (two or three) and a yoga or stretch videotape. Try not to read or listen to the news.
- ✔ Schedule a massage for Saturday. Many cities have massage schools that offer low-cost treatments.
- ✔ Make sure you have bath oils and soothing, relaxing music on hand.

Saturday

- Meditate.
- Have breakfast.
- Go on an early-morning walk (at least 3 to 5 miles). Try to walk in an area that's quiet and peaceful.
- Do yoga or stretching exercises.
- Have a light lunch.
- Take a nap.
- Take a Beauty break.
- Have a massage.
- Enjoy a candlelight dinner. Put on relaxing music. Light candles.
- Watch a videotape or read your book.
- Take a warm soothing bath. Again, light candles and put on relaxing music.
- Meditate and drift off to sleep.

Sunday

- Meditate.
- Watch an inspirational videotape in bed or read.
- Do yoga or stretching exercises.
- Have a light lunch.
- Take a long walk. Practice Silence and Solitude.
- Take a nap.
- Write love letters to friends. Express gratitude for their friendship and love.
- Have an early candlelight dinner.
- Watch a videotape or read.
- Meditate.
- Express gratitude for the weekend and for the good things happening to you.
- Go to bed early.

Whatever form of escape that you choose, try to "get away" into a stress-free, nurturing environment at least once a quarter. This is different from a regular vacation. Noisy, crowded places can wreck havoc with your nerves and consume a lot of energy.

Planning a relaxation and renewal weekend helps to refill the well. After a weekend "away," you'll feel rested, recharged, and ready to take on the world. Enjoy!